Careers in Focus

AUTOMOTIVES

Ferguson

An imprint of Infobase Publishing

Careers in Focus: Automotives

Copyright © 2009 by Infobase Publishing

Ferguson
An imprint of Infobase Publishing
132 West 31st Street
New York NY 10001

Library of Congress Cataloging-in-Publication Data

Careers in focus. Automotives.
    p. cm.
    Includes bibliographical references and index.
    ISBN-13: 978-0-8160-7300-9 (alk. paper)
    ISBN-10: 0-8160-7300-7 (alk. paper)
    1. Automobile industry and trade—Vocational guidance—Juvenile literature.
I. J.G. Ferguson Publishing Company. II. Title: Automotives.
    HD9710.A2C265 2008
    629.222023—dc22
                              2008032092

Ferguson books are available at special discounts when purchased in bulk quantities for businesses, associations, institutions, or sales promotions. Please call our Special Sales Department in New York at (212) 967-8800 or (800) 322-8755.

You can find Ferguson on the World Wide Web at http://www.fergpubco.com

Text design by David Strelecky
Cover design by Salvatore Luongo

Printed in the United States of America

Sheridan MSRF 10 9 8 7 6 5 4 3 2 1

This book is printed on acid-free paper.

Table of Contents

Introduction

The modern automotive industry is massive, complex, and in a continual state of flux. The successful manufacturing of an automobile today—from drawing board to salesroom floor—depends equally upon the expertise of many different professions. There are numerous employment opportunities. If you really want to work in the automotive industry, whether it be in a business, technical, scientific, creative, financial, sales, mechanical, or assembly position, chances are there's a spot for your specialty in or related to the industry.

Careers in automotives offer a great range of earnings potential and educational requirements. Earnings range from slightly more than minimum wage for precision machinists to $100,000 or more for very experienced and successful sales managers, service technicians, engineers, designers, test drivers, and dealership owners. A few of these careers—such as automobile sales worker and automotive industry worker—require little formal education, but are excellent starting points for a career in the industry. Others, such as automobile collision repairer, engineering technician, and automobile detailer, require some postsecondary training or an associate's degree. Many positions in the industry (such as engineer, designer, and sales manager) require a minimum of a bachelor's degree. Advanced degrees—especially for science and engineering careers—are usually required for the best positions.

Approximately 1.1 million people are employed in the motor vehicle and parts manufacturing industry, according to the U.S. Department of Labor. The largest automotive employers in the United States are known as the Big Three (Ford Motor Company, General Motors, and Chrysler LLC). Major Asian and some European automakers also contribute significantly to U.S. industry employment by opening plants in the United States. These include Honda, Nissan, Kia, Toyota, Isuzu, Subaru, Hyundai, BMW, Volkswagen, and Mercedes-Benz.

New and used automotive dealers also offer major job opportunities in the field—employing approximately 1.2 million workers in sales, management, installation, repair, maintenance, and administrative occupations.

The U.S. Department of Labor predicts that employment in the motor vehicle and parts manufacturing industry will decline by 14 percent through 2016 due to increasing competition from international automobile manufacturers, improvements in productivity, and more foreign outsourcing of parts. Employment at automobile dealerships is expected to grow as fast as the average for all industries through 2016, as the number of cars and trucks on U.S. roads is expected to continue to increase.

Much of the recent recovery attempts in the U.S. automotive industry have been characterized by cost-cutting measures, including further elimination of manufacturing jobs and consolidation of large companies. Such mergers often result in the elimination of jobs where efforts would be duplicated under the new organization. Further cuts have also come as American automakers implement lean production measures used by their foreign competitors. Lean production is characterized by increased automation, quality control by workers on the line, and smaller, just-in-time inventories.

Competition among U.S. automakers and their international competitors will be fierce as the Big Three attempt to lure back aging baby boomers from their foreign automobiles, while both battle over capturing younger markets.

Research and development (R&D) is one area where job prospects are expected to remain strong. Major industry players are currently funding billions of dollars each year in R&D and are likely to continue doing so. Fierce competition forces automakers to produce cars packed with new technology, from amenities to safety features, one step above their rival's. A major area of competition is in the development of hybrid electric vehicles—automobiles that combine an electric engine with internal combustion. Hybrids have better fuel economy and create lower pollution emissions than conventional vehicles. Other alternative fuel technologies, such as ethanol and biobutanols, are also being explored. R&D jobs will be mostly for engineers and scientists in the industry. Stricter air pollution laws are also spurring R&D to rethink how cars are powered.

The automotive industry is strongly affected by the health of the economy. A 10 to 20 percent change in employment from one year to the next is not unusual. Less consumer demand for cars and trucks during economic recession usually results in manufacturers firing or laying off workers. Workers with advanced training and education will have the best employment opportunities.

Each article in this book discusses a particular automotive industry occupation in detail. The articles in *Careers in Focus: Automotives* appear in Ferguson's *Encyclopedia of Careers and Vocational Guidance,* but have been updated and revised with the latest information from the U.S. Department of Labor, professional organizations, and other sources. In addition, the following new articles have been written specifically for this book: Automotive Dealership Owners and Sales Managers; Automotive Designers; Automotive Engineering Technicians; Automotive Engineers; Driving School Owners and Instructors; Teachers, Automotive Training; Test Drivers; and Writers, Automotives.

The following paragraphs detail the sections and features that appear in the book.

The **Quick Facts** section provides a brief summary of the career including recommended school subjects, personal skills, work environment, minimum educational requirements, salary ranges, certification or licensing requirements, and employment outlook. This section also provides acronyms and identification numbers for the following government classification indexes: the *Dictionary of Occupational Titles* (DOT), the *Guide for Occupational Exploration* (GOE), the National Occupational Classification (NOC) Index, and the Occupational Information Network (O*NET)-Standard Occupational Classification System (SOC) index. The DOT, GOE, and O*NET-SOC indexes have been created by the U.S. government; the NOC index is Canada's career classification system. Readers can use the identification numbers listed in the Quick Facts section to access further information about a career. Print editions of the DOT (*Dictionary of Occupational Titles*. Indianapolis, Ind.: JIST Works, 1991) and GOE (*Guide for Occupational Exploration*. Indianapolis, Ind.: JIST Works, 2001) are available at libraries. Electronic versions of the NOC (http://www23.hrdc-drhc.gc.ca) and O*NET-SOC (http://online.onetcenter.org) are available on the Internet. When no DOT, GOE, NOC, or O*NET-SOC numbers are present, this means that the U.S. Department of Labor or Human Resources Development Canada have not created a numerical designation for this career. In this instance, you will see the acronym "N/A," or not available.

The **Overview** section is a brief introductory description of the duties and responsibilities involved in this career. Oftentimes, a career may have a variety of job titles. When this is the case, alternative career titles are presented. Employment statistics are also provided, when available. The **History** section describes the history of the particular job as it relates to the overall development of its industry or field. **The Job** describes the primary and secondary duties of the occupation. **Requirements** discusses high school and postsecondary education and training requirements, any certification or licensing that is necessary, and other personal requirements for success in the job. **Exploring** offers suggestions on how to gain experience in or knowledge of the particular job before making a firm educational and financial commitment. The focus is on what can be done while still in high school (or in the early years of college) to gain a better understanding of the job. The **Employers** section gives an overview of typical places of employment for the job. **Starting Out** discusses the best ways to land that first job, be it through the college career services office, newspaper ads, Internet employment sites, or personal contact. The **Advancement** section describes what kind of career path to expect from the job and how to get there. **Earnings** lists salary ranges and describes the typical fringe benefits. The **Work Environment** section describes the typical surroundings and conditions of employment—whether indoors or outdoors, noisy or quiet, social or independent. Also discussed are typical hours worked, any seasonal fluctuations, and the stresses and strains of the job. The **Outlook** section summarizes the job in terms of the general economy and industry projections. For the most part, Outlook information is obtained from the U.S. Bureau of Labor Statistics and is supplemented by information gathered from professional associations. Job growth terms follow those used in the *Occupational Outlook Handbook*. Growth described as "much faster than the average" means an increase of 21 percent or more. Growth described as "faster than the average" means an increase of 14 to 20 percent. Growth described as "about as fast as the average" means an increase of 7 to 13 percent. Growth described as "more slowly than the average" means an increase of 3 to 6 percent. "Little or no change" means a decrease of 2 percent to an increase of 2 percent. "Decline" means a decrease of 3 percent or more. Each article ends with **For More Information**, which lists organizations that provide information on training, education, internships, scholarships, and job placement.

Careers in Focus: Automotives also includes photographs, informative sidebars, and interviews with professionals in the field.

Automobile Collision Repairers

OVERVIEW

Automobile collision repairers repair, replace, and repaint damaged body parts of automobiles, buses, and light trucks. They use hand and power tools to straighten bent frames and body sections, replace badly damaged parts, smooth out minor dents and creases, remove rust, fill small holes or dents, and repaint surfaces damaged by accident or wear. Some repairers also provide repair estimates. Approximately 179,200 automobile collision repairers are working in the United States, plus 26,800 automotive glass specialists and 773,000 general auto mechanics.

HISTORY

The proliferation of the automobile in American society in the 1920s meant new opportunities for many who had not traveled far beyond their hometown. It also created something else by the thousands—jobs. One profession necessitated by America's new love for automobiles was that of the collision repairer. With ill-prepared roads suddenly overrun by inexperienced drivers, accidents and breakdowns became a common problem.

Automobiles were significantly simpler in the early years. Body repairs often could be performed by the owner or someone with a general mechanical aptitude. Minor body dents, if they did not affect driving, were usually left alone. As cars became more complex and as society grew ever more fond of their automobiles, the need for qualified collision repairers grew. Automobiles suddenly became major status symbols, and people were no longer indifferent to minor dents and fender-benders. To many, dents were intolerable. New body styles and materials made body repairs a difficult job. To meet this new demand, some automobile mechanics shifted their focus from repairs under the hood to repairs to the body of automobiles.

By the 1950s, automobile body repair garages were common in cities throughout the United States. More drivers carried vehicle insurance to protect against loss due to an accident. The insurance industry began to work more closely with automobile collision repairers. Since traffic control methods and driving rules and regulations were not very well established, frequent car accidents kept these repair garages busy year-round. Most collision repairers learned the trade through hands-on experience as an apprentice or on their own through trial and error. When automakers began packing their cars with new technology, involving complex electrical circuitry, computer-controlled mechanisms, and new materials, as well as basic design changes, collision repairers found themselves in need of comprehensive training.

THE JOB

Automobile collision repairers repair the damage vehicles sustain in traffic accidents and through normal wear. Repairers straighten bent bodies, remove dents, and replace parts that are beyond repair. Just as a variety of skills are needed to build an automobile, so a range of skills is needed to repair body damage to vehicles. Some body repairers specialize in certain areas, such as painting, welding, glass replacement, or air bag replacement. All collision repairers should know how to perform common repairs, such as realigning vehicle frames, smoothing dents, and removing and replacing panels.

Vehicle bodies are made from a wide array of materials, including steel, aluminum, metal alloys, fiberglass, and plastic, with each material requiring a different repair technique. Most repairers can work with all of these materials, but as car manufacturers produce vehicles with an increasing proportion of lightweight fiberglass, aluminum, and plastic parts, more repairers specialize in repairing these specific materials.

Collision repairers frequently must remove car seats, accessories, electrical components, hydraulic windows, dashboards, and trim to get to the parts that need repair. If the frame or a body section of the vehicle has been bent or twisted, frame repairers and straighteners can sometimes restore it to its original alignment and shape. This is done by chaining or clamping it to an alignment machine, which uses hydraulic pressure to pull the damaged metal into position. Repairers use specialty measuring equipment to set all components, such as engine parts, wheels, headlights, and body parts, at manufacturer's specifications.

After the frame is straightened, the repairer can begin to work on the car body. Newer composite car bodies often have "panels" that can be individually replaced. Dents in a metal car body can be corrected in several different ways, depending on how deep they are. If any part is too badly damaged to repair, the collision repairers remove it with hand tools, a pneumatic metal-cutting gun, or acetylene torch, and then weld on a replacement. Some dents can be pushed out with hydraulic jacks, pneumatic hammers, prying bars, and other hand tools. To smooth small dents and creases, collision repairers may position small anvils, called dolly blocks, against one side of the dented metal. They then hit the opposite side of the metal with various specially designed hammers. Tiny pits and dimples are removed with pick hammers and punches. Dents that cannot be corrected with this treatment may be filled with solder or a putty-like material that becomes hard like metal after it cures. When the filler has hardened, collision repairers file, grind, and sand the surface smooth in the correct contour and prepare it for painting. In many shops the final sanding and painting are done by other specialists, who may be called *automotive painters*.

Since more than the body is usually damaged in a major automobile accident, repairers have other components to repair. Advanced vehicle systems on new cars such as antilock brakes, air bags, and other "passive restraint systems" require special training to repair. Steering and suspension, electrical components, and glass are often damaged and require repair, removal, or replacement.

Automotive painting is a highly skilled, labor-intensive job that requires a fine eye and attention to detail for the result to match the preaccident condition. Some paint jobs require that less than the whole vehicle be painted. In this case, the painter must mix pigments to match the original color. Although this can be difficult if the original paint is faded, today's computer technology is making paint matching easier.

A major part of the automobile collision repairer's job is assessing the damage and providing an estimate on the cost to repair it. Sometimes, the damage to a vehicle may cost more to repair than the vehicle is worth. When this happens, the vehicle is said to be "totaled," a term used by collision repairers as well as insurance companies. Many body repair shops offer towing services and will

Key Skills for Success

Diane Rodenhouse is the owner of Rodenhouse Body Shop in Grand Rapids, Michigan. The shop has been in business for more than 55 years. The editors of *Careers in Focus: Automotives* asked Diane to detail the skills that young people need to be successful in collision repair.

To be successful in their careers, young people need to place as many tools in their "toolbox" as possible. These tools include the following:

- English grammar. You need to have the ability to communicate accurately and professionally in an email or letter.
- Chemistry. There are many paint formulas and chemicals in a collision shop. A basic understanding of how to handle these products and how they work adds value to your toolbox.
- Math. The tool of math can make or break your net profit. For example, how do you figure the cost of the repairs? Body shops usually work by commission. How do you figure your wages? Part discounts and mark up—how do you do the math?
- Computer skills. The paint mixing system, the frame machine, the estimating programs are all done via computer software.

The collision repair industry is a complex, high-skilled profession. Every day is filled with new challenges and opportunities to learn and add to your toolbox of life. There is a shortage of young people entering the collision repair industry. If you study to fill your toolbox and are willing to work responsibly, you will be very successful in the collision industry.

coordinate the transfer of a vehicle from the accident scene as well as the transfer of a totaled vehicle to a scrap dealer who will salvage the useable parts.

The shop supervisor or repair service estimator prepares the estimate. They inspect the extent of the damage to determine if the vehicle can be repaired or must be replaced. They note the year, model, and make of the car to determine type and availability of parts. Based on past experience with similar types of repair and general industry guidelines, estimates are calculated for parts and labor and then submitted to the customer's insurance company. One "walk around" a car will tell the collision repairer what needs to be investigated. Since a collision often involves "hidden" damage, supervisors write up repair orders with specific instructions so no work is missed or, in some cases, done unnecessarily. Repair orders often indicate only specific parts are to be repaired or replaced. Collision repairers generally work on a project by themselves with minimal supervision. In large, busy shops, repairers may be assisted by helpers or apprentices.

REQUIREMENTS

High School

Technology demands more from the collision repairer than it did 10 years ago. In addition to automotive and shop classes, high school students should take mathematics, English, and computer classes. Adjustments and repairs to many car components require numerous computations for which good mathematics skills are essential. Reading comprehension skills will help a collision repairer understand complex repair manuals and trade journals that detail new technology. Oral communication skills are also important to help customers understand their options. In addition, computers are common in most collision repair shops. They keep track of customer histories and parts and often detail repair procedures. Use of computers in repair shops will only increase in the future, so students will benefit from a basic knowledge of them.

Postsecondary Training

A wide variety of training programs are offered by community colleges, vocational schools, independent organizations, and manufacturers. As automotive technology changes, the materials and methods involved in repair work change. With new high-strength steels, aluminum, and plastics becoming ever more common in newer vehicles and posing new challenges in vehicle repair, repairers will need special training to detect the many hidden problems that occur beyond the impact spot. Postsecondary training programs provide students with the necessary, up-to-date skills needed for repairing today's vehicles.

Certification or Licensing

Collision repairers may be certified by the National Institute for Automotive Service Excellence. Although certification is voluntary, it is a widely recognized standard of achievement for automobile collision repairers and the way many advance. Collision repairers who are certified are more valuable to their employers than those who are not and therefore stand a greater chance of advancement.

Other Requirements

Automobile collision repairers are responsible for providing their own hand tools at an investment of approximately $6,000 to $20,000 or more, depending on the technician's specialty. It is the employer's responsibility to provide the larger power tools and other test equipment. Skill in handling both hand and power tools is essential for any repairer. Since each collision repair job is unique and presents a different challenge, repairers often must be resourceful in their method of repair.

While union membership is not a requirement for collision repairers, many belong to the International Association of Machinists and Aerospace Workers; International Union, United Automobile, Aerospace and Agricultural Implement Workers of America; Sheet Metal Workers International Association; or International Brotherhood of Teamsters. Most collision repairers who are union members work for large automobile dealers, trucking companies, and bus lines.

EXPLORING

Many community colleges and park districts offer general auto maintenance, mechanics, and body repair workshops where students can get additional practice working on real cars and learn from experienced instructors. Trade magazines such as *Automotive Body Repair News* (http://www.abrn.com) are excellent sources for learning what's new in the industry. Such publications may be available at larger public libraries or vocational schools. Many journals also post current and archived articles on the Internet. In addition, the Inter-Industry Conference on Auto Collision Repair offers a useful career exploration site, http://collisioncareers.org.

Working on cars as a hobby provides invaluable firsthand experience in repair work. A part-time job in a repair shop or dealership allows a feel for the general atmosphere and the kind of problems repairers face on the job as well as a chance to learn from those already in the business.

Some high school students may gain exposure to automotive repairs through participation in organizations, such as SkillsUSA (http://www.skillsusa.org). SkillsUSA coordinates competitions in several vocational areas, including collision repair. The collision repair competition tests students' aptitudes in metal work, metal inert gas (MIG) welding, painting, alignment of body and frame, painting, estimation of damage to automobiles, and plastic identification and repair. SkillsUSA is represented in all 50 states. If your school does not have a SkillsUSA chapter, ask your guidance counselor about starting one or participating in a co-op arrangement with another school.

EMPLOYERS

Automobile collision repairers hold about 179,200 jobs in the United States, not including 26,800 glass specialists and 773,000 general service technicians and mechanics. Most work for body shops specializing in body repairs and painting, including private shops and facilities operated by automobile dealers. Others work for organizations that maintain their own vehicle fleets, such as trucking companies and automobile rental companies. More than 15 percent of automobile collision repairers are self-employed, operating small shops in cities large and small.

STARTING OUT

The best way to start out in the field of automobile collision repair is, first, to attend one of the many postsecondary training programs available throughout the country and, second, to obtain certification. Trade and technical schools usually provide job placement assistance for their graduates. Schools often have contacts with local employers who seek highly skilled entry-level employees. Often, employers post job openings at nearby trade schools with accredited programs.

Although postsecondary training programs are considered the best way to enter the field, some repairers learn the trade on the job as apprentices. Their training consists of working for several years under the guidance of experienced repairers. Fewer employers today are willing to hire apprentices because of the time and cost it takes to train them, but with the current shortage of high-quality, entry-level collision repair technicians, many employers will continue to hire apprentices who can demonstrate good mechanical aptitude and a willingness to learn. Those who do learn their skills on the job will inevitably require some formal training if they wish to advance and stay in step with the changing industry.

Internship programs sponsored by car manufacturers or independent organizations provide students with excellent opportunities to actually work with prospective employers. Internships can also provide valuable contacts who will be able to refer the student to future employers and provide a recommendation to potential employers once they have completed their training. Many students may even be hired by the company at which they interned.

ADVANCEMENT

With today's complex automobile components and new materials requiring hundreds of hours of study and practice to master, employers encourage their workers to advance in responsibility by learning new systems and repair procedures. A repair shop's reputation will only go as far as its employees are skilled. Those with good communications and planning skills may advance to shop supervisor or service manager at larger repair shops or dealerships. Those who have mastered collision repair may go on to teaching at postsecondary schools or work for certification agencies.

EARNINGS

Salary ranges of collision repairers vary depending on level of experience, type of shop, and geographic location. The median annual salary for automotive body and related repairers was $35,180 in 2006, according to the U.S. Department of Labor. At the lower end of the pay scale, repairers with less experience and repairers who were employed by smaller shops tended to earn less; experienced repairers with management positions earned more. The lowest paid 10 percent earned $21,000 or less, and the top 10 percent earned $59,720 or more. In many repair shops and dealerships, collision repairers can make more by working on commission, typically earning 40 to 50 percent of the labor costs charged to customers. Employers often guarantee a minimum level of pay in addition to commissions.

Benefits packages vary from business to business. Most repair technicians can expect health insurance and a paid vacation from employers. Other benefits may include dental and eye care, life and disability insurance, and a pension plan. Employers usually cover a technician's work clothes and may pay a percentage of the cost of hand tools they purchase. An increasing number of employers pay all or most of an employee's certification training, dependent on the employee passing the test. A technician's salary can increase through yearly bonuses or profit sharing if the business does well.

WORK ENVIRONMENT

Collision repair work is generally noisy, dusty, and dirty. In some cases, the noise and dirt levels have decreased as new technology such as computers and electrostatic paint guns are introduced. Automobile repair shops are usually well ventilated to reduce dust and dangerous fumes. Because repairers weld and handle hot or jagged pieces of metal and broken glass, they wear safety glasses, masks, and protective gloves. Minor hand and back injuries are the most common problems. When reaching in hard-to-get-at places or loosening tight bolts, collision repairers often bruise, cut, or burn their hands. With caution and experience, most learn to avoid hand injuries. Working for long periods in cramped or bent positions often results in a stiff back or neck. Collision repairers also lift many heavy objects that can cause injury if not handled carefully; however, this is less of a problem with new cars as automakers design smaller and lighter parts for better fuel economy. Automotive painters wear respirators and other protective gear, and they work in specially ventilated rooms to keep from being exposed to paint fumes and other hazardous chemicals. Painters may need to stand for hours at a time as they work.

By following safety procedures and learning how to avoid typical problems, repairers can minimize the risks involved in this job. Likewise, shops must comply with strict safety procedures to help employees avoid accident or injury. Collision repairers are often under pressure to complete the job quickly. Most repairers work a standard 40-hour week but may be required to work longer hours when the shop is busy or in handling emergencies.

OUTLOOK

Like many service industries, the collision repair industry is facing a labor shortage of skilled, entry-level workers in many areas of the country. Demand for collision repair services is expected to remain strong, as the number of cars in the nation grows, and employment opportunities are expected to increase about as fast as the average for all occupations through 2016. This demand, paired with technology that will require new skills, translates into a healthy job market for those willing to undergo the training needed. According to *Automotive Body Repair News,* as the need for skilled labor is rising, the number of people pursuing collision repair careers is declining. In many cases, vocational schools and employers are teaming up to recruit new workers.

Changing technology also plays a role in the industry's outlook. New automobile designs have body parts made of steel alloys, aluminum, and plastics—materials that are more time consuming to work with. In many cases, such materials are more prone to damage, increasing the need for body repairs.

The automobile collision repair business is not greatly affected by changes in economic conditions. Major body damage must be repaired to keep a vehicle in safe operating condition. During an economic downturn, however, people tend to postpone minor repairs until their budgets can accommodate the expense. Nevertheless, body repairers are seldom laid off. Instead, when business is bad, employers hire fewer new workers. During a recession, inexperienced workers face strong competition for entry-level jobs. People with formal training in repair work and automobile mechanics are likely to have the best job prospects in such times.

The best employment prospects will be found at automotive body, paint, interior, and glass repair shops. Little employment change is expected at automotive dealerships. Faster-than-average employment growth is predicted for automotive glass installers and repairers.

FOR MORE INFORMATION

For information on scholarships, contact
Automotive Aftermarket Industry Association
7101 Wisconsin Avenue, NW, Suite 1300
Bethesda, MD 20814-3415
Tel: 301-654-6664
Email: aaia@aftermarket.org
http://www.aftermarket.org

For information on training opportunities, contact
Inter-Industry Conference on Auto Collision Repair
5125 Trillium Boulevard
Hoffman Estates, IL 60192-3600
Tel: 800-422-7872
http://www.i-car.com and http://ed-foundation.org

For information on accredited training programs, contact
National Automotive Technicians Education Foundation
101 Blue Seal Drive, Suite 101
Leesburg, VA 20175-5646
Tel: 703-669-6650
http://www.natef.org

For information on certification, contact
National Institute for Automotive Service Excellence
101 Blue Seal Drive, SE, Suite 101
Leesburg, VA 20175-5646
Tel: 888-ASE-TEST
http://www.asecert.org

For information on careers, visit
Automotive Careers Today
http://www.autocareerstoday.net

INTERVIEW

Steve Garrett is an instructor of automotive collision technology at Indian Hills Community College (http://www.ihcc.cc.ia.us) in Iowa. He discussed the field with the editors of Careers in Focus: Automotives.

Q. Tell us about your college's program and your background.

A. The Indian Hills Community College Automotive Collision Technology program is an 18-month, six-term program that covers such topics as air-conditioning, welding, sheet metal fundamentals, application of fillers, detailing, glass, mechanical repairs, frame and unibody damage analysis, plastic repair, steering/suspension, estimating, and refinishing—from introduction to advanced. Successfully completing these courses along with related arts and sciences courses will reward a graduate with an associate of applied science degree.

As for my background, I was exposed to the auto body business at an early age through friends of my dad. I was fascinated with the ability to make a beat-up vehicle look new again. In high school I took an introductory class in auto body during my junior year and a half-day vocational class in my senior year. The next step was to enroll in the auto body program at Indian Hills, which was a one-year diploma program at that time.

Eventually I went to work at a high production collision repair shop in Kansas City, then a General Motors dealership body shop. At that point I decided it was time to try making a living on my own. After about four years, the dealership that I had worked for offered me the manager's position. That was a very valuable experience and during that time I strengthened my relationship with Indian Hills, which led to the opportunity to become an instructor.

Q. What is one thing that young people may not know about a career in automotive collision repair technology?

A. Because of the continual changes in vehicle systems and construction methods, ongoing training is required. Many employers encourage their technicians to participate in industry training courses by offering bonuses and advancement based on their achievements.

Q. What made you want to become an automotive collision repair technology teacher?

A. When I started in this career I had no intention of being an instructor. Through involvement with the Indian Hills Community College advisory committee for auto collision, I realized a desire to pass on this skill. I also felt it was a good direction to advance my career.

Q. What advice would you offer automotive collision repair technology majors as they graduate and look for jobs?

A. First of all, I would advise you to pursue an education at a reputable vo-tech college where you could improve your skills and receive a degree and credits, although many high schools offer top-quality courses that may be sufficient for employment. Hopefully, by the time you graduate, you have decided that this is the career that you desire. If so, be sure to maintain a passion for this business, be critical of yourself in the quality of work you do, and present yourself as the professional you are.

Q. What are the most important personal and professional qualities for teachers?

A. As a teacher in this field of study, it takes a person with very good communication skills and patience. Also, involvement in community activities is important, as well as a good relationship with other industry professionals.

Q. What are the most important personal and professional qualities for automotive collision repair technology majors?

A. Intelligence, like most professions, is a necessary quality. Patience (do you like intricate work?) and an artistic ability are very helpful because shaping body filler is basically sculpting. In addition, repair technicians need to be physically fit.

Q. What is the employment outlook in the field?

A. Career opportunities in automotive collision repair are very good compared to similar skilled trades although an aspiring auto body technician needs to be educated properly in the repair business. I wouldn't say that there is a shortage of technicians, but there is a need for qualified techs.

Automobile Detailers

OVERVIEW

Automobile detailing is the careful cleaning of the interiors and exteriors of cars, vans, boats, and other vehicles. People use the services of a detailing business to keep their vehicles looking new. *Automobile detailers* clean the cars in a commercial shop or at the client's home. They work all across the United States but find the work to be most steady in states where the weather is mild year-round. Approximately 12,000 detail businesses are in operation in the automotive "appearance-care" industry.

HISTORY

Prior to World War I, fewer than a million cars were on the roads and streets of the United States; in the years after, the number grew to five million. By 1925, 20 million cars were in use. About this time, industry pioneer Henry Ford quit producing the Model T because of the growth of the used car market. People could buy better-quality used cars for the same price as the mass-produced Model T. Other car companies met the challenge of the used car market by developing a new version of a familiar model every year.

The used car market, along with the evolution of cars as status symbols, contributed to the development of the car appearance industry. Auto detailers were first hired by used car dealers to prepare run-down or damaged cars for resale. The late 1940s saw the introduction of Turtle Wax (then known as Plastone) and other car care products, as well as the first automatic car washes. The average lifespan of a car in 1971 was a little over five years; now cars last nearly eight. Auto detailers and car care products help keep these longer-lasting cars looking new.

THE JOB

As with other cleaning services, auto detailing is great work for the clean "freak" who also happens to love cars. With some training, a specially equipped van, and a good eye for detail, automobile detailers make old cars look new again and keep new cars looking new. In some cases, they just do a basic wash and vacuum, but in other cases they focus on cleaning every nook and cranny of a car, inside and out. Detailers polish and wax the exterior surface, cleaning and protecting any rubber, trim, glass, and chrome. They also clean the wheels and tires. With the proper equipment, they can sand and buff exterior paint jobs. Inside the car, they vacuum the carpet, treat the vinyl and leather, and clean the dashboard and vents. Detailers attend to stubborn stains on the exterior of the car, like road tar, tree sap, and grease. As a result, they must have an understanding of cleaners and how they work, and they must be creative in dealing with troublesome blotches and blemishes. Though they rely on specially formulated cleaners, they also find some household items useful in getting at stubborn interior stains, items like vinegar (for all-purpose cleaning), cornstarch (for grease and oil), and pencil erasers (for ink and crayon marks).

"Mobile" detailing is when services are performed at clients' homes or office parking lots. Many people prefer the services of a mobile detailing service; having the service come to them eliminates the need for driving to a commercial service and waiting for the car to be cleaned. Through a mobile detailing service, detailers can service corporate fleets of vans, trucks, and even light aircraft.

Anthony Rabak owns a mobile detailing service that serves the areas of Elk Grove, Laguna, and Sacramento, California. With a special cargo van equipped with its own water and power supply, Rabak takes to the streets to attend to his appointments. "I'm the kind of person who pays attention to the little things," Rabak says, "which is very important in detailing. Don't cut corners!"

To ensure that he blasts every speck of dirt and grime, Rabak carries 110 gallons of purified water in his van, along with an electric pressure washer, a 50-foot hose, and a short-nozzle spray gun. "I use purified water because it doesn't leave water spots," he says. "And I chose an electric washer because they are much quieter in a residential area and you can usually plug them into a power source at a location." In case there isn't a power source on site, Rabak has a gas-powered generator and a power inverter.

"Usually I perform most of my work in the shade," he says, "and when there isn't any, I make my own with a portable, folding canopy tent." Rabak's time on site varies according to how much detailing the vehicle owner requests. A basic car wash takes about an hour, while a full detail can take all day.

In addition to the power washer and hose, he uses a simple bucket, car wash soap, and natural sea sponges on the cars' exteriors. "I use the sea sponges because they cause the least amount of scratches," Rabak adds. He also uses towels, special cleaning brushes, and a variety of cleaning chemicals.

With a speed rotary polisher and a dual-head orbital polisher, Rabak can effectively wax paint and scrub carpets. "I also use a shop vacuum with a specially made 15-foot hose and various attachments," he adds. For stubborn carpet and upholstery stains, Rabak uses a shampoo machine, but often he uses just a spray shampoo, scrub brush, and elbow grease.

Some detailers specialize in exotic cars, like Porsches, Jaguars, or Lamborghinis, preparing the cars for shows, races, and other events, while others will clean anything from an RV to a golf cart. Detailers may set up special maintenance contracts with individuals or businesses, regularly servicing vehicles every six or eight weeks. Most individual clients, however, only request detailing services once or twice a year. Detailers who own their own shops may offer more than cleaning. With a garage and employees, a detailer can offer painting, windshield repair, dent removal, leather dying, and other interior and exterior improvements.

REQUIREMENTS

High School

If you are considering owning your own detailing business, take courses that will prepare you for small business ownership. Math and accounting courses will help prepare you for the bookkeeping tasks of the work. You should also take any other business or economic courses that will give you some insight into the job market and the requirements of running a profitable business. Join your high school's business club to learn about business practices and to meet local entrepreneurs.

In addition, while in high school, take English courses to develop communication skills for dealing with clients and promoting your service. Chemistry and shop courses will give you an understanding of the cleansers and equipment you'll be using and also give you practice working with your hands.

Postsecondary Training

Though a college degree isn't required to be a detailer, courses in small business management from a community college will provide knowledge for building your own successful service. Check with a local detailing chain or local garage to see if you can be hired on a training basis. Some companies offer detailing training, such as franchisers Maaco, Ziebart, or National Detail Systems.

Certification or Licensing

Detailers do not need to be certified, a fact that has many professional detailers concerned. A survey by *Professional Carwashing and Detailing* magazine found that 88 percent of respondents have had to fix finishes harmed by another careless detailer. Whether any kind of regulation comes in the future depends on the International Carwash Association.

If detailers plan to run their own business, they will be required to obtain a local business license. In addition, some cities and states also require special licenses for mobile service work.

Other Requirements

Purchasing the equipment to start a mobile detailing service is fairly inexpensive. As a result, it is important that detailers be very professional and dedicated to their customers. Any bad word-of-mouth can hurt business, sending potential customers to one of many competitors. "People are comfortable when I arrive in a clean, organized service vehicle," Anthony Rabak says. Rabak also wears a uniform and is always polite to his clients. "I show that I have an interest in them as a person, and not just their car. People like to have a relationship with individuals who provide services for them," he says.

As with any small business, detailers are entirely responsible for their own success. They must be ambitious, disciplined, and self-motivated to seek out clients and schedule their own work hours. They must also be capable of budgeting their money for months when business may be slow.

Finally, detailers have to keep up-to-date on the latest cleansers and treatments. Improvements are made continuously to cleaning materials and procedures to battle harsh conditions that affect cars, such as acid rain and chemicals used to clean and clear streets.

EXPLORING

Cleaning a car well requires more than a hose and a bucket; but even without all the proper equipment, you can learn much about cleansers and their effect on a car simply by washing the family vehicle. Learn on your own, for example, how to clean a windshield without leaving streaks or how to best remove stains from interior carpets and upholstery.

Rabak explored the job through research. "I read every book on automobile detailing I could find at the library and bookstores," he says. "I talked with detailing supply distributors."

Spend a few days with a local detailer with a good reputation to get a sense of the job. Interview detailers in your area to find out what equipment they use, how much they charge, and how many hours they work. *Professional Carwashing and Detailing Online* (http://www.carwash.com) features many articles on the business as well as a bulletin board for industry professionals.

EMPLOYERS

A number of companies that sell supplies and equipment also offer franchise opportunities. By franchising with a detail chain like Ziebart or National Detail Systems, you'll receive discounts, phone support, and marketing assistance. But be very careful selecting a company to work with; some operations sell equipment at a very large price and offer very little support. Check with the International Carwash Association or consult *Professional Carwashing and Detailing* magazine for reputable companies.

Many detailers are their own employers. Either as owners of a detailing shop or their own mobile business, independent detailers with a solid client base do very well for themselves.

STARTING OUT

Books on detailing and other research can give you an idea of the equipment detailers need to start out. Before buying, be sure to price-shop the supply and equipment distributors for the best deals. Starting out, detailers need about $500 to pay for an electric buffer, a shop vacuum, and the polishes, waxes, and other cleaning chemicals. Due to the high cost of water tanks, Anthony Rabak rents one.

It took a while for Rabak to get his business going. He tried traditional advertising, including a listing in the Yellow Pages, but none of it produced much interest. Eventually word got around that he did good work, and business picked up. "The best results," he says, "have come from word-of-mouth. People who were happy with my work, showed their cars to others, and highly recommended me."

ADVANCEMENT

If an automobile detailer's business has taken off, he or she may feel the need to hire employees and purchase more vans to serve more customers. Some detailing services contract with utility companies, police departments, car dealerships, and other clients with large numbers of vehicles to clean regularly.

Detailers working for an employer may choose to open their own shop. As their new business grows, they may choose to expand the number of services offered. Many detailers offer painting and minor collision repair in addition to cleaning services. They may also do special pinstriping, upholstery repair, and convertible top replacement.

EARNINGS

Cleaners of vehicles and equipment at automobile dealers earned median annual salaries of $19,302 in 2006, according to the U.S. Department of Labor.

The revenue for an automobile detailing establishment depends on the size of the business, operating costs, number of employees, location, years in the business, and many other factors. Obviously, a single-operator mobile detailing service won't have as many customers as a large, multiple-bay car wash and detailing business. According to National Detail Systems, mobile detailers can make anywhere from $35 to $55 per hour, charging between $45 and $65 for a basic detail, depending on the size of the vehicle. A more comprehensive detail can cost between $100 to $140, depending on the condition of the vehicle.

Benefits for full-time workers include vacation and sick time, health, and sometimes dental, insurance, and pension or 401(k) plans. Self-employed automobile detailers are responsible for providing their own benefits.

WORK ENVIRONMENT

Automobile detailers work mostly on their own without much supervision. Their work, however, may be carefully scrutinized by customers expecting their cars to shine like new. "It's a great feeling when you see how pleased and amazed people are with your work," Anthony Rabak says.

The work can be physically demanding, requiring some crawling around and bending; detailers also spend a lot of time on their feet. In some cases, they use harsh chemicals that may irritate skin and any allergies. Most detailing work is done outside, unless detailers own a shop where some services will be performed in the garage. Therefore, weather conditions greatly affect their work.

Rabak charges by the hour. However, between driving to and from appointments and doing the bookkeeping and scheduling, there are many hours for which he isn't paid. "You're responsible for all aspects of your business," Rabak says. "You are the public relations director, advertiser, receptionist, secretary, file clerk, etc."

Detailers can, however, set their own hours, scheduling appointments only for the days they choose. But they have to work as regularly as possible during the spring and summer months if living in an area with cold winters.

OUTLOOK

Some auto industry experts predict that the year 2030 will see a billion cars on the streets of the world. On average, people are spending more and more time in their cars than ever before. As a result, they have more of an incentive to take good care of their cars—helping business for automobile detailers. The longer lifespans and higher value of cars will also increase the demand for detailing professionals. Vehicles, on average, are now built to last longer—and they are not getting any cheaper. Therefore, people should continue to hire detailers to help keep their older cars looking new.

The mobile detailer will especially benefit from the growing number of double-income couples. With hectic schedules and more disposable income, working professionals prefer mobile detailing services that cater to their availability, rather than having to drive to a service and sit in line for hours.

FOR MORE INFORMATION

To learn more about the car wash and detailing industry, such as consumer car washing attitudes and habits, contact
International Carwash Association
401 North Michigan Avenue
Chicago, IL 60611-4255
Tel: 888-ICA-8422

Email: info@CarCareCentral.com
http://www.carcarecentral.com

For information on training programs and answers to frequently asked questions about the profession, contact
National Detail Systems
9452 Telephone Road, Suite 175
Ventura, CA 93004-2600
Tel: 800-356-9485
Email: nds@nationaldetail.com
http://www.nationaldetail.com

To learn more about the current issues affecting car washing and detailing, visit Professional Carwashing and Detailing Online, *or write to the address below for subscription information.*
Professional Carwashing and Detailing
NTP Media
13 Century Hill Drive
Latham, NY 12110-2113
Tel: 518-783-1281
http://www.carwash.com

Automobile Sales Workers

OVERVIEW

Automobile sales workers inform customers about new or used automobiles, and they prepare payment, financing, and insurance papers for customers who have purchased a vehicle. It is their job to persuade the customer that the product they are selling is the best choice. They prospect new customers by mail, telephone, or personal contacts. To stay informed about their products, sales workers regularly attend training sessions about the vehicles they sell. Approximately 280,000 automobile sales workers are employed in the United States.

HISTORY

By the 1920s, nearly 20,000 automobile dealerships dotted the American landscape as the Big Three automobile makers—Ford, General Motors, and Chrysler—increased production every year to meet the public's growing demand for automobiles. Automobile sales workers began to earn higher and higher wages. As automobiles became more popular, the need for an organization to represent the growing industry became evident. In 1917, the National Automobile Dealers Association (NADA) was founded to change the way Congress viewed automobiles. In the early years, NADA worked to convince Congress that cars weren't a luxury item, as they had been classified, but vital to the economy. The group prevented the government from converting all automotive factories to wartime work during

World War I and reduced a proposed luxury tax on automobiles from 5 to 3 percent.

During the lean years of the Depression in the early 1930s, automobile sales fell sharply until President Franklin Delano Roosevelt's New Deal helped jumpstart the industry. Roosevelt signed the Code of Fair Competition for the Motor Vehicle Retailing Trade, which established standards in the automotive manufacturing and sales industries. By 1942, the number of dealerships in the United States more than doubled to 44,000.

Automobile sales workers have suffered an image problem for much of the career's history. Customers sometimes felt that they were pressured to purchase new cars at unfair prices and that the dealer's profit was too large. The 1958 Price Labeling Law, which mandated cars display window stickers listing manufacturer suggested retail prices and other information, helped ease relations between sales workers and their customers. However, in the fiercely competitive automobile market, sales workers' selling methods and the thrifty customer remained at odds.

When it came to used vehicles, there was no way for customers to know whether they were getting a fair deal. Even in the automobile's early history, used vehicles have been popular. From 1919 through the 1950s, used car sales consistently exceeded new car sales. Despite the popularity of used vehicles, the automobile sales industry didn't quite know how to handle them. Some dealers lost money on trade-ins when they stayed on the lot too long. After debating for years how to handle trade-ins, dealers finally began today's common practice of applying their value toward down payments on new cars.

The industry suffered personnel shortages when the armed forces recruited mechanics during World War II. This affected the service departments of dealerships, which traditionally have generated the biggest profits, and many dealers had to be creative to stay in business. During these lean times, sales gimmicks, such as giveaways and contests, came into increased use. According to a history of NADA, one Indiana dealer bought radios, refrigerators, freezers, and furnaces to sell in his showroom and sold toys at Christmas to stay in business.

The energy crisis of the 1970s brought hard times to the entire automotive industry. Many dealerships were forced to close, and those that survived made little profit. In 1979 alone, 600 dealerships closed. As of 2006, according to NADA, there were 21,200 dealerships nationwide (down from 47,500 in 1951) accounting for about 14 percent of all retail sales and employing more than 1.2 million people. Most dealerships today sell more makes of cars than dealerships of the past. Still, they face competition from newer forms of automobile retailers, such as automotive superstores, the automotive equivalent to discount stores like Wal-Mart. Also, automotive information is becoming more widely available on the Internet, eroding the consumer's need for automobile sales workers as a source of information about automobiles.

THE JOB

The automobile sales worker's main task is to sell. Today, many dealerships try to soften the image of salepeople by emphasizing no pressure, even one-price shopping. But automobile dealers expect their employees to sell, and selling in most cases involves some degree of persuasion. The automobile sales worker informs customers of everything there is to know about a particular vehicle. A good sales worker finds out what the customer wants or needs and suggests automobiles that may fit that need—empowering the customer with choice and a feeling that he or she is getting a fair deal.

Since the sticker price on new cars is only a starting point to be bargained down, and since many customers come to dealerships already knowing which car they would like to buy, sales workers spend much of their time negotiating the final selling price.

Most dealerships have special sales forces for new cars, used cars, trucks, recreational vehicles, and leasing operations. In each specialty, sales workers learn all aspects of the product they must sell. They may attend information and training seminars sponsored by manufacturers. New car sales workers, especially, are constantly learning new car features. Sales workers inform customers about a car's performance, fuel economy, safety features, and luxuries or accessories. They are able to talk about innovations over previous models, engine and mechanical specifications, ease of handling, and ergonomic designs. Good sales workers also keep track of competing models' features.

In many ways, used car sales workers have a more daunting mass of information to keep track of. Whereas new car sales workers concentrate on the most current features of an automobile, used car sales workers must keep track of all features from several model years. Good used car dealers can look at a car and note immediately its make, model, and year. Because of popular two- and three-year leasing options, the used car market has increased by nearly 50 percent in the last 10 years.

Successful sales workers are generally good readers of a person's character. They can determine exactly what it is a customer is looking for in a new car. They must be friendly and understanding of customers' needs to put them at ease (due to the amount of money involved, car buying is an unpleasant task for most people). They are careful not to oversell the car by providing the customers with information they may not care about or understand, thus confusing them. For example, if a customer only cares about style, sales workers will not impress upon him all of the wonderful intricacies of a new high-tech engine design.

Sales workers greet customers and ask if they have any questions about a particular model. It's very important for sales workers to have immediate and confident answers to all questions about the vehicles they're selling. When a sale is difficult, they occasionally use psychological methods, or subtle "prodding," to influence customers. Some sales workers use aggressive selling methods and pressure the customer to purchase the car. Although recent trends are turning away from the pressure-sell, competition will keep these types of selling methods prevalent in the industry, albeit at a slightly toned-down level.

Customers usually make more than one visit to a dealership before purchasing a new or used car. Because one salesperson "works" the customer on the first visit—forming an acquaintanceship and learning the customer's personality—he or she will usually stay with that customer until the sale is made or lost. The sales worker usually schedules time for the customer to come in and talk more about the car in order to stay with the customer through the process and not lose the sale to another salesperson. Sales workers may follow up with phone calls to offer special promotions or remind customers of certain features that make a particular model better than the competition, or they may send mailings for the same purpose.

In addition to providing the customer with information about the car, sales workers discuss financing packages, leasing options, and warranties. When the sale is made, they review the contract with the customer and obtain a signature. Frequently the exact model with all of the features the customer requested is not in the dealership, and the sales worker must place an order with the manufacturer or distributor. When purchasing a new or used vehicle, many customers trade in their old one. Sales workers appraise the trade-in and offer a price.

At some dealerships sales workers also do public relations and marketing work. They establish promotions to get customers into their showrooms, print fliers to distribute in the local community, and make television or radio advertisements. To keep their name

An automobile sales worker (left) explains a vehicle's features to a customer. *(Bob Daemmrich, The Image Works)*

in the back (or front) of the customer's mind, they may send past customers birthday and holiday cards or similar "courtesies." Most larger dealerships also have an auto maintenance and repair service department. Sales workers may help customers establish a periodic maintenance schedule or suggest repair work.

Computers are used at a growing number of dealerships. Customers use computers to answer questions they may have, consult price indexes, check on ready availability of parts, and even compare the car they're interested in with the competition's equivalent. Although computers can't replace human interaction and sell the car to customers who need reassurances, they do help the customer feel more informed and more in control when buying a car.

Internet sales specialists are sales workers who specialize in selling vehicles at a dealership's Web site. They manage Internet sales leads and answer customers' questions. They work with webmasters to keep the dealership's Web site up-to-date and attractive to potential buyers. Internet sales specialists help develop special Web-only sales and promotions and ensure that the latest and most comprehensive information is posted. They also arrange test drives and schedule deliveries of vehicles that have been purchased on the Web by customers.

REQUIREMENTS

High School

Because thorough knowledge of automobiles—from how they work to how they drive and how they are manufactured—is essential for a successful sales worker, automotive maintenance classes in high school are an excellent place to begin. Classes in English, speech, drama, and psychology will help you to achieve the excellent speaking skills you will need to make a good sale and gain customer confidence and respect. Classes in business and mathematics will teach you to manage and prioritize your workload, prepare goals, and work confidently with customer financing packages. As computers become increasingly prevalent in every aspect of the industry, you should take as many computer classes as you can. Speaking a second language will give you an advantage, especially in major cities with large minority populations.

Postsecondary Training

Those who seek management-level positions will have a distinct advantage if they possess a college degree, preferably in business or marketing, but other degrees, whether in English, economics, or psychology, are no less important, so long as applicants have good management skills and can sell cars. Many schools offer degrees in automotive marketing and automotive aftermarket management that prepare students to take high-level management positions. Even with a two- or four-year degree in hand, many dealerships may not begin new hires directly as managers, but first start them out as sales workers.

Certification or Licensing

By completing the certified automotive merchandiser program offered by the NADA, students seeking entry-level positions gain a significant advantage. Certification assures employers that workers have the basic skills they require.

Other Requirements

In today's competitive job market, you will need a high school diploma to land a job that offers growth possibilities, a good salary, and challenges; this includes jobs in the automobile sales industry. Employers prefer to hire entry-level employees who have had some previous experience in automotive services or in retail sales. They look for candidates who have good verbal, business, mathematics, electronics, and computer skills. A number of automotive sales and services courses and degrees are offered by community colleges, vocational schools, independent organizations, and manufacturers. Sales workers should possess a valid driver's license and have a good driving record.

Sales workers must be enthusiastic, well-organized self-starters who thrive in a competitive environment. They must show excitement and authority about each type of car they sell and convince customers, without being too pushy (though some pressure on the customer usually helps make the sale), that the car they're interested in is the "right" car, at the fairest price. Sales workers must be able to read a customer's personality and know when to be outgoing and when to pull back and be more reserved. A neat, professional appearance is also very important for sales workers.

EXPLORING

Automobile trade magazines and books, in addition to selling technique and business books, are excellent sources of information for someone considering a career in this field. Local and state automobile and truck dealer associations can also provide you with information on career possibilities in vehicle sales. Your local Yellow Pages has a listing under "associations" for dealer organizations in your area.

Students interested in automobile sales work might first stop by their local dealer and ask about training programs and job requirements there. On a busy day at any dealership several sales workers will be on the floor selling cars. Students can witness the basic selling process by going to dealerships and unobtrusively watching and listening as sales workers talk with customers. Many dealerships hire students part time to wash and clean cars. This is a good way to see the types of challenges and pressures automobile sales workers experience every day. Although it may take a special kind of sales skill or a different approach to sell a $25,000 vehicle over $50 shoes, any type of retail sales job that requires frequent interaction with customers will prepare students for work as an automobile sales worker.

EMPLOYERS

Approximately 280,000 automobile sales workers are employed in the United States. Franchised automobile dealerships, dealers that are formally recognized and authorized by the manufacturer to sell its vehicles, employ the majority of automobile sales workers in the United States. A small number of sales workers are employed by used car dealerships that are strictly independent and not recognized by any manufacturer. Automotive superstores need automobile sales workers as well, although some may argue that these workers aren't truly automobile sales specialists because they tend to have less training and experience in the automotive area.

STARTING OUT

Generally, those just out of high school are not going to land a job as an automobile sales worker; older customers do not feel comfortable making such a large investment through a teenager. Employers prefer to see some previous automotive service experience with certification, such as National Institute for Automotive Service Excellence certification, or postsecondary training in automotive selling, such as NADA's CAM program. Dealerships will hire those with proven sales skill in a different field for sales worker positions and give them on-the-job training.

Employers frequently post job openings at schools that provide postsecondary education in business administration or automotive marketing. Certified automotive technicians or body repairers who think they might eventually like to break into a sales job should look for employment at dealership service centers. They will have frequent contact with sales workers and make connections with dealership managers and owners, as well as become so familiar with one or more models of a manufacturer's cars that they will make well-informed, knowledgeable sales workers. You can also visit http://www.showroomtoday.com for job listings and advice on career development.

Some dealerships will hire young workers with little experience in automobile services but who can demonstrate proven skills in sales and a willingness to learn. These workers will learn on the job. They may first be given administrative tasks. Eventually they will accompany experienced sales workers on the showroom floor and learn "hands-on." After about a year, the workers will sell on their own, and managers will evaluate their selling skills in sales meetings and suggest ways they can improve their sales records.

ADVANCEMENT

The longer sales workers stay with a dealership, the larger their client base grows and the more cars are sold. Advancement for many sales workers comes in the form of increased earnings and customer loyalty. Other sales workers may be promoted through a combination of experience and further training or certification.

As positions open, sales workers with proven management skills go on to be assistant and general managers. Managers with excellent sales skills and a good client base may open a new franchise dealership or their own independent dealership.

The Society of Automotive Sales Professionals (SASP), a division of NADA, provides sales workers with advancement possibilities. Once sales workers have completed a certification process and have a minimum of six months' sales experience, they are eligible to participate in SASP seminars that stress improving the new car buying process by polishing a sales worker's professional image.

EARNINGS

Earnings for automobile sales workers vary depending on location, size, and method of salary. Previously, most dealerships paid their sales workers either straight commission or salary plus commission. This forced sales workers to become extremely aggressive in their selling strategy—and often too aggressive for many customers. With a new trend toward pressure-free selling, more sales workers are earning a straight salary. Many dealerships still offer incentives such as bonuses and profit sharing to encourage sales. The average hourly wage for automotive sales workers was $18.70 in 2006, according to the U.S. Department of Labor. This makes for an annual salary of approximately $38,896 a year. Those who work on a straight commission basis can earn more; however, their earnings are minimal during slow periods. Sales workers who are just getting started in the field may earn lower annual salaries for a few years as they work to establish a client base. They may start in the low $20,000s. According to Automotive Retailing Today, a coalition of all major automobile manufacturers and dealer organizations, automobile sales workers earn salaries that range from $30,000 to $92,000.

Benefits vary by dealership but often include health insurance and a paid vacation. An increasing number of employers will pay all or most of an employee's certification training.

WORK ENVIRONMENT

Sales workers for new car dealerships work in pleasant indoor showrooms. Most used car dealerships keep the majority of their cars in outdoor lots where sales workers may spend much of their day. Upon final arrangements for a sale, they work in comfortable office spaces at a desk. Suits are the standard attire. During slow periods, when competition among dealers is fierce, sales workers often work under pressure. They must not allow "lost" sales to discourage their work. The typical workweek is between 40 and 50 hours, although if business is good, a sales worker will work more. Since most customers shop for cars on the weekends and in the evenings, work hours are irregular.

OUTLOOK

Automobile dealerships are one of the businesses most severely affected by economic recession. Conversely, when the economy is strong, the automobile sales industry tends to benefit. For the sales worker, growth, in any percentage, is good news, as they are the so-called front-line professionals in the industry who are responsible for representing the dealerships and manufacturers and for getting their cars out on the streets. In the late 1990s and early 2000s, automobile sales were especially strong in the United States; however, a weak economy in recent years has caused some setbacks.

The automobile sales worker faces many future challenges. A shift in customer buying preferences and experience is forcing sales workers to reevaluate their selling methods. Information readily available on the Internet helps customers shop for the most competitive financing or leasing package and read reviews on car and truck models that interest them. Transactions are still brokered at the dealer, but once consumers become more familiar with the Internet, many will shop and buy exclusively from home.

Another trend threatening dealers is the automotive superstores, such as CarMax and AutoNation, where customers have a large inventory to select from at a base price and get information and ask questions about a car not from a sales worker, but from a computer. Sales workers are still needed to finalize the sale, but their traditional role at the dealership is lessened.

Nonetheless, the number of cars and trucks on U.S. roads is expected to increase, and opportunities in this lucrative, but stressful, career should continue to increase about as fast as the average.

FOR MORE INFORMATION

For industry information, contact
American International Automobile Dealers
211 North Union Street, Suite 300
Alexandria, VA 22314-2643
Tel: 800-GO-AIADA
http://www.aiada.org

For information on accreditation and testing, contact
National Automobile Dealers Association
8400 Westpark Drive
McLean, VA 22102-5116
Tel: 800-252-6232
Email: nadainfo@nada.org
http://www.nada.org

For information on certification, contact
National Institute for Automotive Service Excellence
101 Blue Seal Drive, SE, Suite 101
Leesburg, VA 20175-5646
Tel: 877-273-8324
http://www.asecert.org

For information on careers, visit
Automotive Careers Today
http://www.autocareerstoday.net

Automobile Service Technicians

QUICK FACTS

School Subjects
Business
Technical/shop

Personal Skills
Mechanical/manipulative
Technical/scientific

Work Environment
Primarily indoors
Primarily one location

Minimum Education Level
High school diploma

Salary Range
$19,070 to $33,780 to
$100,000+

Certification or Licensing
Recommended

Outlook
Faster than the average

DOT
620

GOE
05.03.01

NOC
7321

O*NET-SOC
49-3023.00

OVERVIEW

Automobile service technicians maintain and repair cars, vans, small trucks, and other vehicles. Using both hand tools and specialized diagnostic test equipment, they pinpoint problems and make the necessary repairs or adjustments. In addition to performing complex and difficult repairs, technicians perform a number of routine maintenance procedures, such as oil changes, tire rotation, and battery replacement. Technicians interact frequently with customers to explain repair procedures and discuss maintenance needs. Approximately 773,000 automotive service technicians work in the United States.

HISTORY

By the mid-1920s, the automobile industry began to change America. As automobiles changed through the years, mechanics—or automobile service technicians, as they are now called—have kept them running. The Big Three automobile makers—Ford, General Motors, and Chrysler—produced millions of cars for a public eager for the freedom and mobility the automobile promised. With the ill-prepared roads suddenly overrun by inexperienced drivers, accidents and breakdowns became common. People not only were unskilled in driving but also were ignorant of the basic maintenance and service the automobile required. It suddenly became apparent that a new profession was in the making.

Already in 1899 the American Motor Company opened a garage in New York and advertised "competent mechanics always on hand to make repairs when necessary." Gradually, other repair "garages" opened in larger cities, but they were few and far between. Automobiles were much simpler in the early years. Basic maintenance and minor repairs often could be performed by the owner or someone with general mechanical aptitude.

As cars became more complex, the need for qualified technicians grew. Dealerships began to hire mechanics to handle increasing customer concerns and complaints. Gas stations also began to offer repair and maintenance services. The profession of automobile mechanic was suddenly in big demand.

By the 1950s, automobile service and repair garages were common throughout the United States, in urban and rural areas alike. Most mechanics learned the trade through hands-on experience as an apprentice or on their own through trial and error. When automakers began packing their cars with new technology, involving complex electrical circuitry, and computer-controlled mechanisms as well as basic design changes, it became apparent that mechanics would need comprehensive training to learn new service and repair procedures. Until the 1970s, there was no standard by which automobile service technicians were trained. In 1972, the National Institute for Automotive Service Excellence (ASE) was established. It set national training standards for new technicians and provided continuing education and certification for existing technicians when new technology became widespread in the field.

Today, the demand for trained, highly skilled professionals in the service industry is more important than ever. To keep up with the technology that is continually incorporated in new vehicles, service technicians require more intensive training than in the past. Today, mechanics who have completed a high level of formal training are generally called automobile service technicians. They have studied the complexities of the latest automotive technology, from computerized mechanisms in the engine to specialized diagnostic testing equipment.

THE JOB

Many automobile service technicians feel that the most exciting part of their work is troubleshooting—locating the source of a problem and successfully fixing it. Diagnosing mechanical, electrical, and computer-related troubles requires a broad knowledge of how cars work, the ability to make accurate observations, and the patience to logically determine what went wrong. Technicians agree that it frequently is more difficult to find the problem than it is to fix it. With experience, knowing where to look for problems becomes second nature.

There are two types of automobile service technicians: *generalists* and *specialists*. Generalists work under a broad umbrella of repair and service duties. They have proficiency in several kinds of light repairs and maintenance of many different types of automobiles. Their work, for the most part, is routine and basic. Specialists concentrate in one or two areas and learn to master them for many different car makes and models. Today, in light of the sophisticated technology common in new cars, there is an increasing demand for specialists. Automotive systems are not as easy or as standard as they used to be, and they now require many hours of experience to master. To gain a broad knowledge in auto maintenance and repair, specialists usually begin as generalists.

When a car does not operate properly, the owner brings it to a service technician and describes the problem. At a dealership or larger shop, the customer may talk with a *repair service estimator*, who writes down the customer's description of the problem and relays it to the service technician. The technician may test-drive the car or use diagnostic equipment, such as motor analyzers, spark plug testers, or compression gauges, to determine the problem. If a customer explains that the car's automatic transmission does not shift gears at the right times, the technician must know how the functioning of the transmission depends on the engine vacuum, the throttle pressure, and—more common in newer cars—the onboard computer. Each factor must be thoroughly checked. With each test, clues help the technician pinpoint the cause of the malfunction. After successfully diagnosing the problem, the technician makes the necessary adjustments or repairs. If a part is too badly damaged or worn to be repaired, the technician replaces it after first consulting the car owner, explaining the problem, and estimating the cost.

Normal use of an automobile inevitably causes wear and deterioration of parts. Generalist automobile technicians handle many of the routine maintenance tasks to help keep a car in optimal operating condition. They change oil, lubricate parts, and adjust or replace components of any of the car's systems that might cause a malfunction, including belts, hoses, spark plugs, brakes, filters, and transmission and coolant fluids.

Technicians who specialize in the service of specific parts usually work in large shops with multiple departments, car diagnostic centers, franchised auto service shops, or small independent operations that concentrate on a particular type of repair work.

Tune-up technicians evaluate and correct engine performance and fuel economy. They use diagnostic equipment and other computerized devices to locate malfunctions in fuel, ignition, and emissions-control systems. They adjust ignition timing and valves and may replace spark plugs, points, triggering assemblies in electronic ignitions, and other components to ensure maximum engine efficiency.

Electrical-systems technicians have been in healthy demand in recent years. They service and repair the complex electrical and computer circuitry common in today's automobile. They use both sophisticated diagnostic equipment and simpler devices such as ammeters, ohmmeters, and voltmeters to locate system malfunctions. In addition to possessing excellent electrical skills, electrical-systems technicians require basic mechanical aptitude to get at electrical and computer circuitry located throughout the automobile.

Front-end technicians are concerned with suspension and steering systems. They inspect, repair, and replace front-end parts (such as springs and shock absorbers) and linkage parts (such as tie rods and ball joints). They also align and balance wheels.

Brake repairers work on drum and disk braking systems, parking brakes, and their hydraulic systems. They inspect, adjust, remove, repair, and reinstall such items as brake shoes, disk pads, drums, rotors, wheel and master cylinders, and hydraulic fluid lines. Some specialize in both brake and front-end work.

Transmission technicians adjust, repair, and maintain gear trains, couplings, hydraulic pumps, valve bodies, clutch assemblies, and other parts of automatic transmission systems. Transmissions have become complex and highly sophisticated mechanisms in newer model automobiles. Technicians require special training to learn how they function.

Automobile-radiator mechanics clean radiators using caustic solutions. They locate and solder leaks and install new radiator cores. In addition, some radiator mechanics repair car heaters and air conditioners and solder leaks in gas tanks.

Alternative fuel technicians are relatively new additions to the field. This specialty has evolved with the nation's efforts to reduce its dependence on foreign oil by exploring alternative fuels, such as ethanol, biobutanol, and electricity.

As more automobiles rely on a variety of electronic components, technicians have become more proficient in the basics of electronics, even if they are not electronics specialists. Electronic controls and instruments are located in nearly all the systems of today's cars. Many previously mechanical functions in automobiles are being replaced by electronics, significantly altering the way repairs are performed. Diagnosing and correcting problems with electronic components often involves the use of specialty tools and computers.

Automobile service technicians use an array of tools in their everyday work, ranging from simple hand tools to computerized diagnostic equipment. Technicians supply their own hand tools at an investment of $6,000 to $25,000 or more, depending on their specialty. It is usually the employer's responsibility to furnish the larger power tools, engine analyzers, and other test equipment.

To maintain and increase their skills and to keep up with new technology, automobile technicians must regularly read service and repair manuals, shop bulletins, and other publications. They must also be willing to take part in training programs given by manufacturers or at vocational schools. Those who have voluntary certification must periodically retake exams to keep their credentials.

REQUIREMENTS

High School

In today's competitive job market, aspiring automobile service technicians need a high school diploma to land a job that offers growth possibilities, a good salary, and challenges. There is a big push in the automotive service industry to fill entry-level positions with well-trained, highly skilled persons. Technology demands more from the technician than it did 10 years ago.

In high school, you should take automotive and shop classes, mathematics, English, and computer classes. Adjustments and repairs to many car components require the technician to make numerous computations, for which good mathematical skills are essential. Good reading skills are also valuable, as a technician must do a lot of reading to stay competitive in today's job market. English classes will prepare you to handle the many volumes of repair manuals and trade journals you will need to remain informed. Computer skills are also vital, as computers are now common in most repair shops. They keep track of customers' histories and parts and often detail repair procedures. Use of computers in repair shops will only increase in the future.

Postsecondary Training

Employers today prefer to hire only those who have completed some kind of formal training program in automobile mechanics—usually a minimum of two years. A wide variety of such programs are offered by community colleges, vocational schools, independent organizations, and manufacturers. Many community colleges and vocational schools around the country offer accredited postsecondary education. These programs are accredited by the National Automotive Technicians Education Foundation and the Accrediting Commission of Career Schools and Colleges of Technology. Postsecondary training programs prepare students through a blend of classroom instruction and hands-on practical experience. They range in length from six months to two years or more, depending on the type of program. Shorter programs usually involve intensive study. Longer programs typically alternate classroom courses with periods of work experience. Some two-year programs include courses on applied mathematics, reading and writing skills, and business practices and lead to an associate's degree.

Some programs are conducted in association with automobile manufacturers. Students combine work experience with hands-on classroom study of up-to-date equipment and new cars provided by manufacturers. In other programs, students alternate time in the classroom with internships in dealerships or service departments. These students may take up to four years to finish their training,

Books to Read

Curcio, Vincent. *Chrysler: The Life and Times of an Automotive Genius*. New York: Oxford University Press, 2005.

Gilles, Tim. *Automotive Service: Inspection, Maintenance, Repair*. 3d ed. Clifton Park, N.Y.: CENGAGE Delmar Learning, 2007.

Hollembeak, Barry. *Today's Technician: Automotive Electricity and Electronics*. 4th ed. Clifton Park, N.Y.: CENGAGE Delmar Learning, 2006.

Knowles, Don. *Today's Technician: Automotive Suspension and Steering Systems*. 4th ed. Clifton Park, N.Y.: CENGAGE Delmar Learning, 2006.

Lee, Richard S., and Mary Price Lee. *Careers for Car Buffs & Other Freewheeling Types*. 2d ed. New York: McGraw-Hill, 2003.

Matchett, Steve. *The Mechanic's Tale: Life in the Pit-Lanes of Formula One*. London, U.K.: Orion Media, 2002.

Owen, Clifton E. *Today's Technician: Automotive Brake Systems*. 4th ed. Clifton Park, N.Y.: CENGAGE Delmar Learning, 2007.

Schwaller, Anthony E. *Total Automotive Technology*. 4th ed. Clifton Park, N.Y.: CENGAGE Delmar Learning, 2004.

Turner Publishing Company. *Ford Motor Company: The First 100 Years*. Paducah, Ky.: Turner Publishing Company, 2007.

Van Valkenburgh, Paul. *Race Car Engineering & Mechanics*. New York: HP Books, 2004.

but they become familiar with the latest technology and also earn a modest salary.

Certification or Licensing
Automobile service technicians may be certified by the ASE in one of the following eight areas—automatic transmission/transaxle, brakes, electrical/electronic systems, engine performance, engine repair, heating and air-conditioning, manual drivetrain and axles, and suspension and steering. Those who become certified in all eight areas are known as master mechanics. Although certification is voluntary, it is a widely recognized standard of achievement for automobile technicians and is highly valued by many employers. Certification also provides the means and opportunity to advance. To maintain their certification, technicians must retake the examination for their specialties every five years. Many employers only hire ASE-accredited technicians and base salaries on the level of the technicians' accreditation.

Other Requirements
To be a successful automobile service technician, you must be patient and thorough in your work; a shoddy repair job may put the driver's life at risk. You must have excellent troubleshooting skills and be able to logically deduce the cause of system malfunctions.

EXPLORING

Many community centers offer general auto maintenance and mechanics workshops where you can practice working on real cars and learn from instructors. Trade magazines are excellent sources for learning what's new in the industry and can be found at most public libraries or large bookstores. Many public television stations broadcast automobile maintenance and repair programs that can be of help to beginners to see how various types of cars differ.

Working on cars as a hobby provides valuable firsthand experience in the work of a technician. An after-school or weekend part-time job in a repair shop or dealership can give you a feel for the general atmosphere and kinds of problems technicians face on the job. Oil and tire changes, battery and belt replacement, and even pumping gas may be some of the things you will be asked to do on the job; this work will give you valuable experience before you move on to more complex repairs. Experience with vehicle repair work in the armed forces is another way to pursue your interest in this field.

EMPLOYERS

Approximately 773,000 automotive service technicians are employed in the United States. Because the automotive industry is so vast, automobile service technicians have many choices concerning type of shop and geographic location. Automobile repairs are needed all over the country, in large cities as well as rural areas.

The majority of automobile service technicians work for automotive dealers and independent automotive repair shops and gasoline service stations. The field offers a variety of other employment options as well. The U.S. Department of Labor estimates that nearly 17 percent of automobile service technicians are self-employed. Other employers include franchises such as PepBoys and Midas that offer routine repairs and maintenance, and automotive service departments of automotive and home supply stores. Some automobile service technicians maintain fleets for taxicab and automobile leasing companies or for government agencies with large automobile fleets.

Technicians with experience and/or ASE certification certainly have more career choices. Some master mechanics may go on to teach at technical and vocational schools or at community colleges. Others put in many years working for someone else and go into business for themselves after they have gained the experience to handle many types of repairs and oversee other technicians.

STARTING OUT

The best way to start out in this field is to attend one of the many postsecondary training programs available throughout the country. Trade and technical schools usually provide job placement assistance for their graduates. Schools often have contacts with local employers who need to hire well-trained people. Frequently, employers post job openings at nearby trade schools with accredited programs. Job openings are frequently listed on the Internet through regional and national automotive associations or career networks.

A decreasing number of technicians learn the trade on the job as apprentices. Their training consists of working for several years under the guidance of experienced mechanics. Fewer employers today are willing to hire apprentices due to the time and money it takes to train them. Those who do learn their skills on the job will inevitably require some formal training if they wish to advance and stay in step with the changing industry.

Intern programs sponsored by car manufacturers or independent organizations offer students excellent opportunities to actually work with prospective employers. Internships can provide students with valuable contacts who will be able to recommend future employers once they have completed their training. Many students may even be hired by the shop at which they interned.

ADVANCEMENT

With today's complex automobile components requiring hundreds of hours of study and practice to master, more repair shops prefer to hire specialists. Generalist automobile technicians advance as they gain experience and become specialists. Other technicians advance to diesel repair, where the pay may be higher. Those with good communications and planning skills may advance to shop foreman or service manager at large repair shops or to sales workers at dealerships. Master mechanics with good business skills often go into business for themselves and open their own shops.

EARNINGS

Salary ranges for automobile service technicians vary depending on the level of experience, type of shop the technician works in, and geographic location. Generally, technicians who work in small-town, family-owned gas stations earn less than those who work at dealerships and franchises in metropolitan areas.

According to the U.S. Department of Labor, automobile service technicians had median annual salaries of $33,780 ($16.24 an hour) in 2006. The lowest paid 10 percent made less than $19,070 ($9.17 an hour), and the highest paid 10 percent made more than $56,620 ($27.22 an hour). Since most technicians are paid on an hourly basis and frequently work overtime, their salaries can vary significantly. In many repair shops and dealerships, technicians can earn higher incomes by working on commission. Master technicians who work on commission can earn more than $100,000 annually. Employers often guarantee a minimum level of pay in addition to commissions.

Benefit packages vary from business to business. Most technicians receive health insurance and paid vacation days. Additional benefits may include dental, life, and disability insurance and a pension plan. Employers usually pay for a technician's work clothes and may pay a percentage on hand tools purchased. An increasing number of employers pay for all or most of an employee's certification training, if he or she passes the test. A technician's salary can increase through yearly bonuses or profit sharing if the business does well.

WORK ENVIRONMENT

Depending on the size of the shop and whether it's an independent or franchised repair shop, dealership, or private business, automobile technicians work with anywhere from two to 20 other technicians. Most shops are well lighted and well ventilated. They can frequently be noisy with running cars and power tools. Minor hand and back injuries are the most common problems of technicians. When reaching in hard-to-get-at places or loosening tight bolts, technicians often bruise, cut, or burn their hands. With caution and experience most technicians learn to avoid hand injuries. Working for long periods of time in cramped or bent positions often results in a stiff back or neck. Technicians also lift many heavy objects that can cause injury if not handled carefully; however, this is becoming less of a problem with new cars, as automakers design smaller and lighter parts to improve fuel economy. Some technicians may experience allergic reactions to solvents and oils used in cleaning, maintenance, and repair. Shops must comply with strict safety procedures set by the Occupational Safety and Health Administration and Environmental Protection Agency to help employees avoid accidents and injuries.

The U.S. Department of Labor reports that most technicians work a standard 40-hour week, but 30 percent of all technicians work more than 40 hours a week. Some technicians make emergency repairs to stranded automobiles on the roadside during odd hours.

OUTLOOK

With an estimated 147 million vehicles in operation today in the United States, automobile service technicians should feel confident that a good percentage will require servicing and repair. Skilled and highly trained technicians will be in particular demand. Less-skilled workers will face tough competition. The U.S. Department of Labor predicts that this field will grow faster than the average for all occupations through 2016. According to the ASE, even if school enrollments were at maximum capacity, the demand for automobile service technicians still would exceed the supply in the immediate future. As a result, many shops are beginning to recruit employees while they are still in vocational or even high school.

Another concern for the field is the automobile industry's trend toward developing the "maintenance-free" car. Manufacturers are producing high-end cars that require no servicing for their first 100,000 miles. In addition, many new cars are equipped with on-board diagnostics that detect both wear and failure for many of the car's components, eliminating the need for technicians to perform extensive diagnostic tests. Also, parts that are replaced before they completely wear out prevent further damage from occurring to connected parts that are affected by a malfunction or breakdown. Although this will reduce troubleshooting time and the number of overall repairs, the components that need repair will be more costly and require a more experienced (and hence, more expensive) technician.

Most new jobs for technicians will be at independent service dealers, specialty shops, and franchised new car dealers. Because of the increase of specialty shops, fewer gasoline service stations will hire technicians, and many will eliminate repair services completely. Other opportunities will be available at companies or institutions with private fleets (e.g., cab, delivery, and rental companies, and government agencies and police departments).

FOR MORE INFORMATION

For information on accredited training programs, contact
Accrediting Commission of Career Schools and Colleges of Technology
2101 Wilson Boulevard, Suite 302
Arlington, VA 22201-3062
Tel: 703-247-4212
Email: info@accsct.org
http://www.accsct.org

For more information on the automotive service industry, contact
Automotive Aftermarket Industry Association
7101 Wisconsin Avenue, Suite 1300
Bethesda, MD 20814-3415
Tel: 301-654-6664
Email: aaia@aftermarket.org
http://www.aftermarket.org

For industry information and job listings, contact
Automotive Service Association
PO Box 929
Bedford, TX 76095-0929
Tel: 800-272-7467
Email: asainfo@asashop.org
http://www.asashop.org

For information and statistics on automotive dealers, contact
National Automobile Dealers Association
8400 Westpark Drive
McLean, VA 22102-5116
Tel: 800-252-6232
Email: nadainfo@nada.org
http://www.nada.org

For information on certified educational programs, careers, and certification, contact
National Automotive Technicians Education Foundation
101 Blue Seal Drive, Suite 101
Leesburg, VA 20175-5646
Tel: 703-669-6650
http://www.natef.org

For information on certification, contact
National Institute for Automotive Service Excellence
101 Blue Seal Drive, SE, Suite 101
Leesburg, VA 20175-5646
Tel: 703-669-6600
http://www.asecert.org

Automotive Dealership Owners and Sales Managers

QUICK FACTS

School Subjects
Business
Mathematics

Personal Skills
Communication/ideas
Leadership/management

Work Environment
Indoors and outdoors
One location with some
  travel

Minimum Education Level
Some postsecondary training

Salary Range
$50,000 to $117,748 to
  $300,000+

Certification or Licensing
Voluntary (certification)
Required (licensing)

Outlook
About as fast as the average

DOT
290

GOE
10.01.01

NOC
0621, 6421

O*NET-SOC
11-2022.00, 41-2031.00

OVERVIEW

Automotive dealership owners are proprietors of retail businesses that sell cars exclusively from one or two manufacturers. Most dealerships are independently or family-owned franchises of an automotive manufacturer, such as Ford Motor Company or General Motors. In addition to retail services, dealerships provide maintenance services, repair services, and financing. *Sales managers* coordinate and oversee the performance of sales staff so they meet monthly sales quotas set by the dealership.

HISTORY

For as long as there have been automobiles, there have been automotive dealerships and owners and managers that operated them. By 1951, nearly 47,500 automobile dealerships existed in the United States.

Industry consolidation has more than halved this number today, but the 21,200 dealerships nationwide account for about 14 percent of all retail sales in the United States. These dealerships employ more than 1.1 million people.

Many dealership owners and sales managers belong to the National Automobile Dealers Association (NADA), a nearly century-old organization dedicated to promoting the interests of domestic and international automotive dealership owners. Many dealership owners that specialize in

48

import cars belong to the American International Automobile Dealers, an association representing the economic well-being of more than 11,000 international name-plate dealerships.

THE JOB

To give the public easy access to view and purchase their vehicles, automotive manufacturers maintain franchised dealerships throughout the United States. Automotive dealership owners manage the performance of their showroom and sales force, other departments, and act as a liaison between the manufacturer and consumers.

Dealerships are exclusive to a particular automaker, though they may offer cars from different lines. For example, a Ford dealership will have Ford models in its showroom, but may also have separate department and sales force to promote Lincoln, Mercury, or Land Rover models—other automakers operating under the Ford umbrella. Many existing dealerships are family-owned franchises; some have multiple partnerships; others have consolidated dealerships into a chain representing multiple manufacturers.

The dealership owner's primary focus is to keep the showroom and all other departments operating smoothly and profitably. They establish business policies including those relating to inventory, sales and commissions, and financing. Dealership owners determine the operating budget, which will dictate the size and variety of showroom inventory, sales force and support staff, and the setup of the physical building. They also develop seasonal promotions and advertising campaigns, often working with guidelines set by the manufacturer. Several times a year, they must represent the dealership at franchise meetings, where dealers receive training updates and other business support from the manufacturer. They also promote their dealership at automobile conventions and trade shows.

Sales managers help the dealership owner manage the overall performance of the main showroom and staff. The most important responsibility of sales managers is the hiring and training of the showroom's sales force and support staff. Sales managers assign duties and hours to employees, monitor their progress, evaluate their monthly sales performance, implement incentives and sales drives, and promote and increase base salaries or commissions when appropriate. When an employee's performance is lacking, it is the sales manager's duty to identify the problem and suggest needed changes. At times, the sales manager may have the unpleasant task of firing employees.

Many times, a customer will try to negotiate a lower price for a vehicle from a salesperson. The salesperson may try to counter with added price breaks or extra options at no charge. Oftentimes, the salesperson will have to confer with the sales manager regarding extra discounts off the invoice price. The sales manager has final say over financial transactions with a customer, and may also have influence on what financing options to extend to customers. While the best-case sales scenario is to sell a vehicle at its sticker price, salespeople do not mind negotiating price. Sales commissions, monthly quotas, and "kick backs"—commission paid to the dealership from the manufacturer—are incentives to negotiate price to close a sale.

Automotive dealerships also have other departments that are often as profitable as their primary business of selling cars. The service department offers repair and maintenance work for vehicles. Services include periodic tune-ups and systems check-ups and repair, oil changes, brake repair, wheel alignment, and body work. A service department manager may supervise the work and performance of all service workers and technicians. Their duties include hiring and training of service staff, making work schedules, and establishing vehicle service policies and pricing.

The finance and insurance department often generates large profits for a dealership. A finance or insurance manager establishes relationships with financing and insurance companies, and in turn sells these products—auto loans, service contracts, extended warranties, and various credit insurance—to the consumer. This department often works closely with the sales department in offering these products when closing a car sale. The finance and insurance manager oversees the selling of service contracts and insurance policies to new vehicle buyers and arranges financing options for their purchase.

REQUIREMENTS

High School

Business, math, economics, and accounting courses will be the most valuable to you in preparing for business ownership. In addition, you will need to hone your communication skills, which will be essential in establishing relationships with automotive companies and customers. Take computer classes since it is virtually impossible to work in today's business world without knowing how to use a computer or the Web. In addition, take as many automotive classes as possible. Marketing and advertising classes will be especially useful for aspiring sales managers.

Postsecondary Training

As the business environment becomes more competitive, many people in this field are opting for an academic degree as a way of getting more training. A bachelor's program, or at least an associate's degree, emphasizing business communications, marketing, business law, business management, and accounting, should be pursued. Some people choose to get a master's in business administration or other related graduate degree. Special business schools offer a one- or two-year program in business management. Some correspondence schools also offer courses on how to plan and run a business.

Some automobile dealership owners have degrees in sales or marketing; others have degrees in an automotive-related field. Sales managers typically have degrees in marketing, advertising, or a related field.

Aspiring dealership owners should be aware that is quite difficult to obtain a dealership. Many manufacturers often put those interested in becoming a dealer through an intensive training and interview process. General Motors (GM), for example, has aspiring dealers participate in a 12-month training session. Referred to as GM's Academy Program, qualified individuals receive training in such areas as management, operations, and automotive retailing. Candidates must then undergo a thorough interview with GM officials, an assessment of their dealer skills, and a follow-up on available investment funding. Completion of the academy program does not guarantee future dealership opportunities. Manufacturers consider many factors when awarding a new franchise. For example, they take into account the number of existing dealerships that are currently being sold, if approval has been given for the establishment of new dealerships, and the number of qualified candidates already on the waiting list for dealerships.

The National Automobile Dealers Association also offers a comprehensive training program for future dealers and managers. For more information, visit http://www.dealeracademy.org.

Certification or Licensing

The National Independent Automobile Dealers Association offers the certified master dealer designation to used motor vehicle dealers who successfully complete a four-day program. Contact the association for more information.

A business license is a requirement in all states. Individual states or communities may have zoning codes or other regulations specifying what type of business can be located in a particular area. Check

Facts About Dealerships, 2006

- More than 1.2 million full-time workers were employed by automobile dealerships—1.1 million at new car dealerships, and 127,000 workers at used car dealerships.

- Sales and related careers made up 37 percent of jobs at dealerships; installation, maintenance, and repair-related occupations, 26 percent; office and administrative support occupations, 15 percent; and transportation and material moving occupations, 13 percent.

- Approximately 50 percent of workers at dealerships had more than a high school diploma.

- Thirty-seven percent of employees worked more than 40 hours per week.

- The average number of employees at new vehicle dealerships was 53.

- The average annual earnings of employees at new vehicle dealerships was $47,191.

Sources: U.S. Department of Labor, National Automobile Dealers Association

with your state's chamber of commerce or department of revenue for more information on obtaining a license.

Other Requirements

Whatever the experience and training, a dealership owner needs a lot of energy, patience, and fortitude to overcome the slow times and other difficulties involved in running a business. Other important personal characteristics include maturity, creativity, and good business judgment. Business owners also should be able to motivate employees and delegate authority.

Sales managers should have excellent communication and persuasive skills. They should also be organized and able to delegate responsibilities to their employees.

EXPLORING

Most communities have a chamber of commerce whose members usually will be glad to share their insights into the career of a business owner.

Join your high school's business club, a group that may give you the opportunity to meet business leaders in your community. Contact local dealership owners or sales managers and ask them to participate in an information interview. Discuss the pros and cons of business ownership, find out about the owner's educational and professional background, and ask them for general advice.

You can also read industry publications, such as *AutoExec* (http:// www.autoexecmag.com), to learn more about the field.

EMPLOYERS

As of 2006, there were 21,200 dealerships nationwide. Opportunities are available in all 50 states and in towns large and small. Approximately 28,000 sales managers are employed at automobile dealerships in the United States.

STARTING OUT

Few people start their career as an owner. Many start as a manager or in some other position within a dealership. An aspiring dealership owner should anticipate having at least 50 percent of the money needed to start or buy a business. Some people find it helpful to have one or more partners in a business venture.

The position of sales manager is also not typically an entry-level job. Most sales managers start their careers as automobile sales workers or in another position at a dealership. Visit http://www.showroom today.com for job listings and advice on career development.

ADVANCEMENT

Because an owner is by definition the boss, opportunities are limited for advancement. Advancement often takes the form of expansion of an existing business, leading to increased earnings and prestige. Expanding a business also can entail added risk, as it involves increasing operational costs. A successful business owner may be offered an additional dealership or an executive position with an automotive manufacturer.

Sales managers advance by becoming general managers of dealerships, working for larger dealerships, overseeing more staff, selling more expensive and prestigious vehicles, or eventually owning their own dealerships.

EARNINGS

Earnings for dealership owners vary widely and are greatly influenced by the ability of the individual owner, type of vehicles being sold, other services offered, and existing economic conditions. Some dealership owners may earn less than $50,000 a year, while the most successful owners earn $300,000 or more.

General sales managers employed by automobile dealerships earned median salaries of $117,748 in 2005, according to the National Automobile Dealers Association. Salaries for new car sales managers ranged from $84,000 to $110,000, according to Automotive Careers Today, a coalition of all major automobile manufacturers and dealer organizations. Used car sales managers earned $82,000 to $106,000.

Benefits for sales managers depend on the employer; however, they usually include such items as health insurance, retirement or 401(k) plans, and paid vacation days.

WORK ENVIRONMENT

Automotive dealerships are usually open every day except Sunday and major holidays. Any professional working in this industry should expect long hours, especially during the evening and on Saturday. Busy times include the end of the month, when sales quotas are tallied, and during special promotions, such as a holiday or year-end clearance sales. Pressure or competition to sell is common among members of the sales force. At times, dealership owners and managers may have to contend with unsatisfied or difficult customers, or disputes between employees.

Dealership owners and managers work in comfortable office settings, though their days are often hectic and demanding. As head management, they are often in the dealership until closing time—working 60-hour workweeks is not unusual. They often must travel out of town, or sometimes abroad, to attend conferences, trade shows, or to manufacturers' headquarters or assembly plants.

OUTLOOK

Employment at automobile dealers is expected to grow 11 percent through 2016, according to the U.S. Department of Labor—or about as fast as the average for all industries. The automobile sales industry is tightly linked to the U.S. economy. When the economy is strong, more people purchase vehicles. When the economy is weak, people hold off on purchases, which affects employment at automobile dealerships—especially those that sell new vehicles. Employment growth for new car sales managers may be limited as the consolidation of new car dealerships continues. Nearly 67 percent of workers in this field are employed at dealerships with 50 or more employees, according to the U.S. Department of Labor.

FOR MORE INFORMATION

For industry information, contact
American International Automobile Dealers
211 North Union Street, Suite 300
Alexandria, VA 22314-2643
Tel: 800-GO-AIADA
http://www.aiada.org

For information on accreditation and its dealer academy, contact
National Automobile Dealers Association
8400 Westpark Drive
McLean, VA 22102-5116
Tel: 800-252-6232
Email: nadainfo@nada.org
http://www.nada.org

For information on certification, contact
National Independent Automobile Dealers Association
2521 Brown Boulevard
Arlington, TX 76006
Tel: 800-682-3837
http://www.niada.com

For information on careers, visit
Automotive Careers Today
http://www.autocareerstoday.net

Automotive Designers

School Subjects
Art
Mathematics

Personal Skills
Artistic
Technical/scientific

Work Environment
Primarily indoors
Primarily one location

Minimum Education Level
Bachelor's degree

Salary Range
$31,510 to $66,510 to
$125,000+

Certification or Licensing
None available

Outlook
More slowly than the average

DOT
142

GOE
01.04.02

NOC
2252

O*NET-SOC
27-1021.00

OVERVIEW

Automotive designers, also known as *automotive stylists,* are specialized industrial designers who combine their technical knowledge of mechanics, production, and materials with artistic talent to improve the style, appearance, and ergonomic and aerodynamic design of automobiles. They work full time at automobile manufacturers, or may work as consultants. Approximately 48,000 industrial designers are employed in the United States. Only a small percentage are employed in the automotive industry.

HISTORY

Although industrial design as a separate and unique profession did not develop in the United States until the 1920s, it has its origins in colonial America and the industrial revolution. When colonists were faced with having to make their own products rather than relying on imported goods, they learned to modify existing objects and create new ones. As the advent of the industrial revolution drew near, interest in machinery and industry increased.

The industrial revolution brought about the mass production of objects and increased machine manufacturing. As production capabilities grew, a group of entrepreneurs, inventors, and designers emerged. Together, these individuals determined products that could be mass produced and figured out ways to manufacture them.

In the early 1900s, manufactured products—including the Model T, the first mass-produced automobile—were designed to be functional, utilitarian, and easily produced by machines or assembly line workers. Little attention was paid to aesthetics.

Once the novelty of the early automobile began to wear off, consumers grew increasingly dissatisfied with the design and aesthetic appeal of these vehicles. Automobile manufacturers did not initially respond to these complaints. For example, Henry Ford continued to manufacture only one style of car, the Model T, despite criticism that it looked like a tin can. Ford was unconcerned because he sold more cars than anyone else. When General Motors started selling its attractive Chevrolet in 1926, and it outsold the Model T, Ford finally recognized the importance of styling and design.

Advertising convincingly demonstrated the importance of design. Those products with artistic features sold better, and manufacturers realized that design did play an important role both in marketing and manufacturing. By 1927, automotive manufacturers were hiring people solely to advise them on design features. Industrial design came to represent a new profession: The practice of using aesthetic design features to create manufactured goods that were economical, served a specific purpose, and satisfied the psychological needs of consumers. One of the most famous early designers was Harley Earl, who designed the 1927 Cadillac LaSalle, the first car designed by a stylist. In that same year, Earl founded General Motor's Art and Color Department (which became the Styling Section in 1937). He is best known, according to the Industrial Designers Society of America, for creating "dozens of innovative designs including the hardtop convertible, wrap-around windshields, two-tone paint, heavy chrome plating, and tailfins."

In the following decades, automotive manufacturers paid more attention to style and design in an effort to make their products stand out in the marketplace. They began to hire in-house designers and, following the lead of General Motors, established their own design departments. Today, automotive designers play a major role in both designing new automobiles and other vehicles (motorcycles, recreation vehicles, buses, trucks, coaches, and vans) and determining which models may be successful in the marketplace.

THE JOB

When beginning a new project design, automotive designers confer with the manufacturer's product development team to address several issues. What is the theme and concept of the new vehicle?

What are specific functions expected by the manufacturer? What are the expectations of the consumer? Automotive designers take these concerns into consideration as well as the size and shape of the vehicle, its weight, color, and materials used. They also must take into account how this new model will fit into the manufacturer's existing fleet of cars, safety of the vehicle, and cost of the final product.

The design process begins with a model of the exterior design. At Chrysler's Design Institute, designers draw manual sketches of possible designs. They also rely on computer-aided design (CAD) programs and tools to visualize their concepts. CAD technology is useful as it gives designers easy access to modify their sketches, and many CAD programs can communicate instructions to automated production machinery. Mangers from the design department choose from among the ideas of their staff to present to the heads of Chrysler as possible new model designs.

Designers then work with *clay modelers* to make prototypes to better visualize their concepts. Full-scale prototypes of vehicles are often made of a wood or iron base covered in Styrofoam. They are further enhanced with a thick layer of clay or industrial plasticine that can be molded and smoothed using special tools such as the slick—a styling tool with rounded edges. With this prototype, designers and engineers can get a feel for the model's aerodynamic potential. Workers from manufacturing engineering, production, and marketing work closely with designers to ensure the new vehicle design meets their department's specifications.

Some automotive designers focus on the interior specifications of a new model. In this capacity, designers are concerned with the ergonomic placement of controls on the instrument panel, including controls for the overhead lights, doors, and windows. They may tweak designs or placement to address function and aesthetic and ergonomic features of controls—all within the limited space of a car's interior. Designers must adhere to safety standards as established by the government, while at the same time ensuring that the interior design theme meshes with the car's exterior design.

Once the exterior and interior designs of a new model are approved, the designers move on to other details of the car's appearance.

They also research popular trends in color when selecting the paint and finishes made available for the vehicle. Designers also choose interior colors and fabrics and other materials used for seats, dashboard, and trims for the interior of the car.

REQUIREMENTS
High School
In high school, take as many art and computer classes as possible in addition to college preparatory classes in English, social studies, algebra, geometry, and science. Classes in mechanical drawing may be helpful, but drafting skills are being replaced by the ability to use computers to create graphics and manipulate objects. Science classes, such as physics and chemistry, are also becoming more important as automotive designers select materials and components for vehicles and need to have a basic understanding of scientific principles. Shop classes, such as machine shop, metalworking, and woodworking are also useful and provide training in using hand and machine tools.

Postsecondary Training
A bachelor's degree in fine arts, industrial design, or automotive design (often called transportation design) is recommended, although some employers accept diplomas from art schools. Training is offered through art schools, art departments of colleges and universities, and technical colleges. Most bachelor's degree programs require four or five years to complete. Some schools also offer a master's degree, which requires two years of additional study. Often, art schools grant a diploma for three years of study in industrial design. Programs in industrial design are offered by approximately 50 schools accredited (or that are in the process of accreditation) by the National Association of Schools of Art and Design. There are only about 20 schools worldwide that offers courses or programs in automotive design, according to *Car Design News*. Visit its Web site, http://www.cardesignnews.com, for a list of programs.

School programs vary; some focus on engineering and technical work, while others emphasize art background. Certain basic courses are common to every school: two-dimensional design (color theory, spatial organization) and three-dimensional design (abstract sculpture, art structures). Students also have a great deal of studio practice, learning to make models of clay, plaster, wood, and other easily worked materials. Some schools even use metalworking machinery. Technically oriented schools generally require a course in basic engineering. Schools offering degree programs also require courses in English, history, science, and other basic subjects. Such courses as merchandising and business are important for anyone working in a field so closely connected with the consumer. Most schools also offer classes in computer-aided design and computer graphics. One of the most essential skills for success as an automotive designer is the ability to use design software.

Other Requirements

Automotive designers are creative, have artistic ability, and are able to work closely with others in a collaborative style. In general, designers do not crave fame or recognition because designing is a joint project involving the skills of many people. In most cases, automotive designers remain anonymous and behind the scenes. Successful designers can accept criticism and differences of opinion and be open to new ideas.

EXPLORING

An excellent way to uncover an aptitude for design and to gain practical experience in using computers is to take a computer graphics course through an art school, high school continuing education program, technical school, or community college. Some community colleges allow high school students to enroll in classes if no comparable course is offered at the high school level. If no formal training is available, teach yourself how to use a popular graphics software package.

Summer or part-time employment in an industrial design office, or even at an automotive design firm, is a good way to learn more about the profession and what automotive designers do. Another option is to work in an advertising agency or for a market research firm. Although these companies most likely won't have an automotive designer on staff, they will provide exposure to how to study consumer trends and plan marketing promotions.

Pursue hobbies such as sculpting, ceramics, jewelry making, woodworking, and sketching to develop creative and artistic abilities. Reading about industrial and automotive design can also be very beneficial. Publications such as *Car Design News* (http://www.cardesignnews.com), *Automotive Design & Production* (http://www.autofieldguide.com), and *Design News* (http://www.design-news.com) contain many interesting and informative articles that describe different design products, offer profiles of automotive designers, and detail current trends. These magazines can be found at many public libraries. Read books on the history of automotive design to learn about interesting case studies on the development of automobiles.

EMPLOYERS

Approximately 48,000 industrial designers are employed in the United States, but only a small number work in the automotive industry. Some of the major employers of automotive designers are the Big Three U.S. automobile makers (General Motors, Ford Motor Company, and Chrysler LLC) and major foreign automakers that have factories or divisions in the United States (Honda, Nissan, Toyota, Hyundai, Volkswagen, BMW, and Mercedes-Benz).

STARTING OUT

Most employers prefer to hire someone who has a degree or diploma from a college, art school, or technical school. Persons with engineering, architectural, or other scientific backgrounds also have a good chance at entry-level jobs, especially if they have artistic and creative talent. When interviewing for a job, a designer should be prepared to present a portfolio of their work.

Job openings may be listed through a college career services office or in classified ads in newspapers or trade magazines. They can also be found at the Web sites of publications such as *Car Design News* (http://www.cardesignnews.com). Qualified beginners may also apply directly to companies that hire automotive designers.

Several directories listing industrial design firms can be found in most public libraries. In addition, lists of industrial design firms appear periodically in magazines such as *BusinessWeek* and *Engineering News-Record*. Also, a new industrial designer can get a free copy of *Getting an Industrial Design Job* at the Web site (http://www.idsa.org) of the Industrial Designers Society of America.

ADVANCEMENT

Entry-level automotive designers usually begin as assistants to other designers. They do routine work and hold little responsibility for design changes. With experience and the necessary qualifications, the designer may be promoted to a higher-ranking position with major responsibility for design. Experienced designers may be promoted to project managers or move into supervisory positions. Supervisory positions may include overseeing and coordinating the work of several designers, including freelancers and automotive designers at outside agencies. Some senior designers are given a free hand in designing products. With experience, established reputation, and financial backing, some industrial designers decide to open their own consulting firms.

EARNINGS

According to the Industrial Designers Society of America, the average starting salary for all industrial designers is $36,000.

Designers with five years' experience earn an average of $58,000 a year. Senior designers with 10 years' experience earn $73,000. Industrial designers with 19 years or more experience earn average salaries of $125,000. Managers who direct design departments in large companies earn substantially more. Owners or partners of consulting firms have fluctuating incomes, depending on their business for the year.

According to the U.S. Department of Labor, industrial designers employed in motor vehicle parts manufacturing earned mean annual wages of $66,510 in 2006. Salaries for industrial designers employed in all fields ranged from less than $31,510 to $92,970 or more.

Automotive designers usually receive paid vacations and holidays, sick leave, hospitalization and insurance benefits, and pension programs.

WORK ENVIRONMENT

Workplaces for automotive designers vary depending on the stage of their current project. They work in comfortable offices when doing preliminary sketches, when using computerized design programs, or when brainstorming with other industry professionals. However, they may shift to different areas for other design processes, such as studios when building or modifying prototypes. Some travel may be involved when meeting with different fabric or leather vendors or paint distributors. Automotive designers usually work a regular 40-hour week, but longer hours may be required to meet an important project deadline.

OUTLOOK

Employment in the motor vehicle and parts manufacturing industry is predicted to decline by 14 percent through 2016, according to the U.S. Department of Labor (USDL). Despite this outlook, automotive designers will continue to be needed to create new car designs—especially as competition between automotive companies increases. Designers who combine business expertise with an educational background in engineering and computer-aided design will have the best employment prospects.

Employment of all industrial designers is expected to grow about as fast as the average through 2016, according to the USDL.

FOR MORE INFORMATION

For information on opportunities for women in industrial design,
contact

Association of Women Industrial Designers
Old Chelsea Station
PO Box 468
New York, NY 10011
Email: info@awidweb.com
http://www.awidweb.com

For information on careers, educational programs, and a free copy
of Getting an Industrial Design Job, *contact*

Industrial Designers Society of America
45195 Business Court, Suite 250
Dulles, VA 20166-6717
Tel: 703-707-6000
Email: idsa@idsa.org
http://www.idsa.org

For information on accredited design schools, contact

National Association of Schools of Art and Design
11250 Roger Bacon Drive, Suite 21
Reston, VA 20190-5248
Tel: 703-437-0700
Email: info@arts-accredit.org
http://nasad.arts-accredit.org

Automotive Engineering Technicians

QUICK FACTS

School Subjects
Mathematics
Physics

Personal Skills
Following instructions
Technical/scientific

Work Environment
Indoors and outdoors
Primarily multiple locations

Minimum Education Level
Associate's degree

Salary Range
$30,530 to $44,540 to
$77,080+

Certification or Licensing
Voluntary

Outlook
Decline

DOT
003, 007, 012

GOE
02.08.02, 02.08.04

NOC
2132, 2233, 2241

O*NET-SOC
17-3023.00, 17-3026.00,
17-3027.00, 17-3029.00

OVERVIEW

Automotive engineering technicians use their knowledge and skills in engineering, science, and mathematics to help automotive engineers and other professionals in the research and development, quality control, manufacturing, and design of automobiles or specific systems and components. They work for major automotive manufacturers and contractors worldwide. Approximately 15,000 engineering technicians are employed in the motor vehicle and parts manufacturing industry.

HISTORY

Automotive engineering technicians have been valuable members of automotive engineering teams ever since the first automotive engine was designed and built in the 1880s. Technicians assist automotive engineers, scientists, and other workers in a variety of tasks. They bridge the gap between the engineers and designers who design the automobile, and those who manufacture them.

THE JOB

Imagine driving a car that gets 41 mpg, with zero emissions, and fill-ups lasting about 400 miles. It's not a daydream, but rather a reality—Ford's new Edge, the world's first drivable fuel-cell hybrid electric plug-in vehicle. It was realized with the help of automotive engineering technicians working in the company's research and development

An engineering technician monitors a test in the wind tunnel at the Chrysler Technical Center. *(Jim West Photography)*

department. Their duties included recording data, making computations, plotting graphs, and analyzing efficiency results of the model's HySeries Drive powertrain.

Another example of automotive engineering technicians in the automotive industry are those who work in the manufacturing department at Toyota to help test and implement needed modifications in the design of supplemental restraint systems. More commonly known as air bags, automotive engineering technicians use computer-aided design programs, set up and gather results from crash tests, and help draw designs of the machinery needed to make or install air bag systems, including innovative knee air bags.

Automotive engineers cannot implement important innovations and improvements in the industry without the help of automotive engineering technicians. Under the direction of engineers and designers, engineering technicians are instrumental in building, maintaining, and modifying many aspects of the automobile ranging from safer, well-constructed vehicles, more powerful and efficient systems, and durable components and materials. Automotive engineering technicians may specialize according to their assigned department or project. Opportunities are available in chemical, materials, mechanical, industrial, and many other engineering specialties.

REQUIREMENTS

High School

Preparation for this career begins in high school. Although entrance requirements to associate degree programs vary somewhat from school to school, mathematics and physical science form the backbone of a good preparatory curriculum. Classes should include algebra, geometry, science, trigonometry, calculus, chemistry, mechanical drawing, shop, and physics. Because computers have become essential for automotive engineering technicians, computer courses are also important.

English and speech courses provide invaluable experience in improving verbal and written communication skills. Since some technicians go on to become technical writers or teachers, and since all of them need to be able to explain technical matter clearly and concisely, communication skills are important.

Postsecondary Training

Most employers are interested in hiring graduates with at least a two-year degree in automotive engineering technology or a related field. Technical institutes, community colleges, vocational schools, and universities all offer this course of study.

The Technology Accreditation Commission of the Accreditation Board for Engineering and Technology (http://www.abet.org) accredits engineering technology programs.

Some engineering technicians decide to pursue advancement in their field by becoming automotive engineering technologists. Others branch off into research and development or become engineers. These higher-level, higher-paid positions typically require the completion of a bachelor's degree in engineering technology (for engineering technologists) or at least a bachelor's degree in engineering (for technicians interested in becoming research and development engineers).

Certification or Licensing

Many automotive engineering technicians choose to become certified by the National Institute for Certification in Engineering Technologies. To become certified, you must combine a specific amount of job-related experience with a written examination. Certifications are offered at several levels of expertise. Such certification is generally voluntary, although obtaining certification shows a high level of commitment and dedication that employers find highly desirable.

Electronics automotive engineering technicians may obtain voluntary certification from the International Society of Certified Electronics Technicians and the Electronics Technicians Association, International. Certification is regarded as a demonstration of professional dedication, determination, and know-how.

Automotive engineering technicians are encouraged to become affiliated with professional groups, such as the American Society of Certified Engineering Technicians, that offer continuing education sessions for members. Additionally, some engineering technicians may be required to belong to unions.

Other Requirements

Automotive engineering technicians are relied upon for solutions and must express their ideas clearly in speech and in writing. Good communication skills are important for a technician in the writing and presenting of reports and plans. These skills are also important for working alongside other technicians and professionals, people who are often from many different backgrounds and skilled in varying areas of engineering.

Automotive engineering technicians need mathematical and mechanical aptitude. They must understand abstract concepts and apply scientific principles to problems in the shop, laboratory, or work site.

Many tasks assigned to automotive engineering technicians require patience and methodical, persistent work. Good technicians work well with their hands, paying close attention to every detail of a project. Some technicians are bored by the repetitiveness of some tasks, while others enjoy the routine.

Individuals planning to advance beyond the technician's level should be willing to and capable of pursuing some form of higher education.

EXPLORING

If you are interested in a career as an automotive engineering technician, you can gain relevant experience by taking shop courses, joining electronics or radio clubs in school, and assembling electronic equipment with commercial kits.

You should take every opportunity to discuss the field with people working in it. Try to visit a variety of different kinds of engineering facilities—service shops, automotive manufacturing plants, and research laboratories—either through individual visits or through field trips organized by teachers or guidance counselors. These visits will provide a realistic idea of the opportunities in the different areas of the industry. If you enroll in a community college or technical school, you may be able to secure off-quarter or part-time internships with local employers through your school's career services office. Internships are valuable ways to gain experience while still in school.

EMPLOYERS

Approximately 15,000 engineering technicians are employed in the motor vehicle and parts manufacturing industry. Employers include the Big Three U.S. automobile makers (General Motors, Ford Motor Company, and Chrysler LLC), major foreign automakers that have factories or divisions in the United States (Honda, Nissan, Toyota, Hyundai, Volkswagen, BMW, and Mercedes-Benz), as well as any of the thousands of private manufacturing companies.

STARTING OUT

Most technical schools, community colleges, and universities have career services offices. Automobile companies actively recruit employees while they are still in school or are nearing graduation. Because these job services are the primary source of entry-level jobs for automotive engineering technicians, you should check a school's placement rate before making a final decision about which school you attend.

Another way to obtain employment is through direct contact with a particular automotive company such as Ford or Hyundai. It is best to write to the personnel department and include a resume summarizing your education and experience. If the company has an appropriate opening, a company representative will schedule an interview with you. Many excellent public and commercial employment organizations can also help graduates obtain jobs appropriate to their training and experience.

Newspaper want ads and employment services are other methods of getting jobs. Professional or trade magazines often have job listings and can be good sources for job seekers. Professional associations compile information on job openings and publish job lists. For example, the International Society of Certified Electronics Technicians offers lists of job openings around the country at its Web site. Information about job openings can also be found in trade magazines. Professional organizations are also good for networking with other technicians and are up-to-date on industry advancement, changes, and areas of employment.

ADVANCEMENT

As automotive engineering technicians remain with a company, they become more valuable to their employer. Opportunities for advancement are available for automotive engineering technicians who are willing to accept greater responsibilities either by specializing in a specific field, taking on more technically complex assignments, or by assuming supervisory duties. Some technicians advance by moving into technical sales or customer relations. Others pursue advanced education to become automotive engineering technologists or automotive engineers.

EARNINGS

The earnings of automotive engineering technicians vary widely depending on skills and experience, specialty, type of work, geographical location, and other factors. According to the U.S. Department of Labor (USDL), industrial engineering technicians employed in motor vehicle parts manufacturing earned mean annual wages of $44,540 in 2006.

Salaries for all engineering technicians ranged from less than $30,530 to $77,080 or more annually, according to the USDL.

Automotive engineering technicians generally receive premium pay for overtime work on Sundays and holidays and for evening and night shift work. Most employers offer benefits packages that include paid holidays, paid vacations, sick days, and health insurance. Companies may also offer pension and retirement plans, profit sharing, 401(k) plans, tuition assistance programs, and release time for additional education.

WORK ENVIRONMENT

The work environment for automotive engineering technicians varies according to the project at hand. Technicians may meet in comfortable offices when brainstorming with other members of the research and development team. At times, they may travel to factories or manufacturing plants to test vehicles, or monitor the installation of certain systems. The environment at such places is often loud and busy. When working on site, technicians are required to wear protective clothing and safety goggles.

Technicians are often assigned to shift work, averaging 40 hours a week. They may be asked to work extra shifts or longer hours at times, especially when an important manufacturing deadline is approaching.

OUTLOOK

Employment for engineering technicians in motor vehicle and parts manufacturing is expected to decline through 2016, according to the U.S. Department of Labor. Computer-aided design has allowed individual technicians to increase productivity, thereby limiting job growth. Those with training in sophisticated technologies and those with bachelor's degrees in technology-related fields will have the best employment opportunities.

According to the *Occupational Outlook Handbook*, employment of all engineering technicians is expected to increase about as fast as the average for all occupations through 2016.

FOR MORE INFORMATION

Visit the ASEE's precollege Web site for information on engineering and engineering technology careers.
American Society for Engineering Education (ASEE)
1818 N Street, NW, Suite 600
Washington, DC 20036-2479
Tel: 202-331-3500
http://www.asee.org
http://www.engineeringk12.org/students

Contact the society for information on training and certification.
American Society of Certified Engineering Technicians
PO Box 1536
Brandon, MS 39043-1536
Tel: 601-824-8991
Email: general-manager@ascet.org
http://www.ascet.org

This organization offers information on certification and student membership.
Electronics Technicians Association, International
Five Depot Street
Greencastle, IN 46135-8024
Tel: 800-288-3824

Email: eta@eta-i.org
http://www.eta-sda.com

Contact the society for information on certification and student membership.
International Society of Certified Electronics Technicians
3608 Pershing Avenue
Fort Worth, TX 76107-4527
Tel: 817-921-9101
Email: info@iscet.org
http://www.iscet.org

For information on careers, educational programs, and student clubs, contact
Junior Engineering Technical Society
1420 King Street, Suite 405
Alexandria, VA 22314-2794
Tel: 703-548-5387
Email: info@jets.org
http://www.jets.org

For information on certification, contact
National Institute for Certification in Engineering Technologies
1420 King Street
Alexandria, VA 22314-2794
Tel: 888-IS-NICET
http://www.nicet.org

For information on careers in automotive engineering, contact
SAE International
400 Commonwealth Drive
Warrendale, PA 15096-0001
Tel: 877-606-7323
http://automobile.sae.org

Automotive Engineers

OVERVIEW

Automotive engineers are employed by car and truck manufacturers as well as parts suppliers to design and build entire vehicles or individual parts. They may work on the vehicle's engine design, aerodynamics, performance and fuel efficiency, safety features, ergonomics, and more.

HISTORY

In our car-obsessed society, it is difficult to imagine a time without automobiles. Yet just over 110 years ago, there were none. In the late 1880s, inventors were beginning to explore the idea of a self-propelled vehicle. Early experiments used steam to power a vehicle's engine. Two German engineers developed the first internal combustion engine fueled by gasoline. Karl Benz finished the first model in 1885, and Gottlieb Daimler, with the help of a young engineer named Wilhelm Maybach, finished building a similar model in 1886. Others around the world had similar successes in the late 1800s and early 1900s.

The Society of Automobile Engineers (now known as SAE International) was founded in 1905 to serve the professional interests of automotive engineers and function as a venue for discourse regarding the rapidly growing field. Henry Ford, a young engineer, served as the society's first vice president.

Today, automobiles are infinitely more complex than early vehicles such as the Model T, and automotive engineers continue to remain key players in the automotive industry.

THE JOB

Fresh off the assembly line, new car models are faster, more powerful, sleeker, and loaded with every imaginable upgrade option. These new designs and improvements are made possible through the work of automotive engineers. Automotive engineers are responsible for the design, development and manufacturing of automotive vehicles. They have been trained in a variety of engineering specialties, including mechanical, industrial, safety, materials, chemical, and electrical engineering. Automotive engineers further specialize in a specific area of automotive production.

Production engineering. *Production engineers* design entire systems or single components needed for cars to function. Engineers at Ford Motor Company, for example, may be responsible for designing a better suspension system for a new sports utility model that allows for a smoother ride comparable to that of a sedan. Production engineers often work for large automotive manufacturers, but may also find employment with independent engineering firms specializing in automotive components or systems. Hunter Engineering Company, for example, has had great success in designing and patenting many under-car service equipment and systems used by automotive giants such as Chrysler, Ford, and General Motors.

Once a specific system or part is designed, production engineers must test and validate the design, often using a prototype. They coordinate a team of other engineers, technicians, and suppliers to make necessary alterations in the original plan or material. Identifying cost and manufacturing feasibility is another responsibility of production engineers.

Development engineering. *Development engineers* coordinate delivery of a complete automobile to meet the standards of the manufacturer, government, and consumer. They run a battery of tests to ensure the safe and reliable interaction of all systems and components, and implement any needed changes in the design, structure, or materials used. For example, development engineers working at Nissan may test and tweak the design of a new engine so it gives the driver power and quick acceleration, while at the same time delivering good mileage and fuel efficiency. Development engineers may also work on the vehicle's attributes such as its weight, aerodynamic drag, transmission systems, and more. They are also concerned with the car's ergonomic design. For example, heating and cooling systems must work efficiently, and have controls that are easy to use and well placed on the instrument panel. Development engineers are also responsible for many of the alternative fuel cars available on the market today such as hybrid vehicles. Development engineers at Honda are currently perfecting a vehicle with a "clean diesel" engine design that will be available in a few years.

Manufacturing engineers. Engineers working for automotive manufacturers plan and implement the assembly of the entire vehicle. Engineers working for automotive suppliers have the same responsibility for individual parts or systems. *Manufacturing engineers* oversee the design and layout of the equipment, including the workers assigned to the assembly line. They also run tests to ensure the systems and components stay true to quality and are able to stand up to normal wear and tear, and make adjustments as needed. The manufacturing and installation of parts—including interior and exterior trim, materials for seats, and body panels—are just some items that fall under the responsibility of manufacturing engineers. They often collaborate with a team of other engineers, technicians, and test drivers.

REQUIREMENTS

High School
High school students interested in automotive engineering should take a great deal of mathematics, including geometry, trigonometry, calculus, and two years of algebra. They should develop a strong background in physics, chemistry, biology, and computer programming or applications. Because automotive engineers must communicate constantly with other engineers, scientists, clients, and consumers, four years of language arts are essential.

Postsecondary Training
After high school, students should attend a four-year college or university and earn a bachelor's degree in automotive, mechanical, electronics, materials engineering, or a related engineering field. Some engineers major in a science such as physics, computers, or chemistry and then find work applying their science in an engineering field or go to graduate school for a master's or doctorate degree in engineering. Many engineers, no matter their undergraduate major, now pursue advanced degrees in the field.

Certification and Licensing
Many engineers become certified. Certification is a status granted by technical or professional organizations (such as the Society of Manufacturing Engineers) for the purpose of recognizing and documenting an individual's abilities in a specific engineering field.

Licensure as a professional engineer is recommended since an increasing number of employers require it. Even those employers who do not require licensing will view it favorably when considering new hires or when reviewing workers for promotion. Licensing requirements vary from state to state. In general, however, they involve graduating from an accredited school, having four years of work experience, and passing the eight-hour Fundamentals of Engineering exam and the eight-hour Principles and Practice of Engineering exam. Depending on your state, you can take the Fundamentals exam shortly before your graduation from college or after you have received your bachelor's degree. At that point you will be an engineer-in-training. Once you have fulfilled all the licensure requirements, you receive the designation professional engineer. Visit the National Council of Examiners for Engineering and Surveying's Web site, http://www.ncees.org, for more information on licensure.

Other Requirements

Students who are interested in becoming automotive engineers should enjoy solving problems, developing logical plans, and designing things. They should have a strong interest and ability in science and mathematics. Engineers often work on projects in teams, so prospective engineers should be able to work well both alone and with others.

EXPLORING

Perhaps the best way for high school students to explore the field of engineering is by contacting the Junior Engineering Technical Society (JETS). JETS can help students learn about different fields within engineering and can guide students toward science and engineering fairs.

Participation in science and engineering fairs can be an invaluable experience for a high school student interested in automotive engineering. Through these fairs, students learn to do their own research and applications in a variety of engineering fields. Too often, students leave high school with a strong academic background in mathematics and sciences, but have never applied their knowledge to the real world. By developing a project for a fair, students begin to learn how to think like an engineer by creatively using their academic knowledge to solve real-life problems.

EMPLOYERS

Automotive engineers can find employment with one of the Big Three U.S. automobile makers (General Motors, Ford Motor Company, and Chrysler LLC), major foreign automakers that have factories or divisions in the United States (Honda, Nissan, Toyota, Hyundai, BMW, Volkswagen, and Mercedes-Benz), as well as any of the thousands of private manufacturing companies.

Other possibilities for engineers can be found in academia as instructors or researchers or as writers for engineering-oriented publications. Some mechanical engineers work as test drivers for automotive companies and publishers.

STARTING OUT

College and graduate school programs can help newly degreed automotive engineers locate jobs. These schools are often in touch with prospective employers who are in need of engineers. Conferences, trade shows, and engineering career fairs can also be good places for new engineers to begin meeting employers and setting up interviews.

ADVANCEMENT

As automotive engineers gain more experience, they are given greater responsibilities and tougher problems to solve. At this stage, the engineer will be involved in more decision making and independent work. Some engineers advance to become engineering team managers or supervisors of entire projects. They also may enter administrative or sales positions. In addition, many high-level corporate and government executives started out as engineers.

Advancement depends upon experience and education. The more experience automotive engineers get, the more independence and responsibilities they will probably gain; however, an automotive engineer with a bachelor's degree will, in all probability, not make it to the highest levels of the field. Automotive engineers who are interested in going into corporate, industrial, or executive positions often go back to school to earn degrees in law or business.

EARNINGS

Engineers earn some of the highest starting salaries of any career. The National Association of Colleges and Employers reports that in 2007 engineers with a bachelor's degree earned the following starting salaries by specialty: electrical/electronics, $55,292; industrial/manufacturing, $55,067; materials, $56,233; and mechanical, $54,128.

Salaries for engineers in the automotive industry vary by employer, location, experience, and specialty of the engineer. According to the U.S. Department of Labor, industrial engineers employed in motor vehicle parts manufacturing earned mean annual wages of $67,300 in 2006. Mechanical engineers earned $70,090.

Salaries for engineers employed in all fields ranged from less than $46,080 to $120,610 or more.

Automotive engineers who work for a company usually receive benefits such as vacation days, sick leave, health and life insurance, and a savings and pension program. Self-employed engineers must provide their own benefits.

WORK ENVIRONMENT

Automotive engineers do the majority of their work inside an office. They often are assisted by clerical support staff or research and technical staff members located in offices nearby. Many times, automotive engineers are required to spend at least part of their time on a specific work site. They may find themselves at manufacturing sites or on an assembly line to work on special projects, or to oversee the production of a specific component. People interested in becoming automotive engineers should be flexible about work sites and adjust easily to different types of environments. Some travel is expected, especially to manufacturing plants or contractors located abroad, or to attend automobile conventions or trade shows.

Work hours vary, depending at the task or project at hand. Many times, automotive engineers are expected to work late into the night or on weekends to meet manufacturing deadlines. Automotive engineers often work with other engineers, technicians, and assembly line workers, so the ability to communicate ideas and work well as part of a team is important.

OUTLOOK

Employment in the motor vehicle and parts manufacturing industry is predicted to decline by 14 percent through 2016, according to the U.S. Department of Labor (USDL). Improvements in productivity and more foreign outsourcing of parts have reduced opportunities in the field. Despite this prediction, the industry remains one of the largest employers in the United States, and positions will continue to be available as workers retire or leave the field for other reasons. Employment for industrial engineers employed in motor vehicle and parts manufacturing is expected to grow more slowly than the average, and employment of mechanical engineers is expected to experience a steady decline during this same time period.

Employment for all engineers is expected to grow about as fast as the average through 2016, according to the USDL.

Automotive engineers who stay current concerning the latest technologies and remain flexible in regards to type of employer, location, and other factors will most likely find employment for years to come.

FOR MORE INFORMATION

For a list of accredited schools and colleges, contact
Accreditation Board for Engineering and Technology
111 Market Place, Suite 1050
Baltimore, MD 21202-7116
Tel: 410-347-7700
http://www.abet.org

For more information on careers in engineering, contact
American Society for Engineering Education
1818 N Street, NW, Suite 600
Washington, DC 20036-2479
Tel: 202-331-3500
http://www.asee.org and http://www.engineeringk12.org/students

For information on mechanical engineering, contact
American Society of Mechanical Engineers
Three Park Avenue
New York, NY 10016-5990
Tel: 800-843-2763
Email: infocentral@asme.org
http://www.asme.org

For information on engineering careers and students clubs and competitions, contact
Junior Engineering Technical Society
1420 King Street, Suite 405
Alexandria, VA 22314-2794
Tel: 703-548-5387
Email: info@jets.org
http://www.jets.org

For information on licensure and practice areas, contact
National Society of Professional Engineers
1420 King Street
Alexandria, VA 22314-2794
Tel: 703-684-2800
http://www.nspe.org

For information on careers in automotive engineering, contact
SAE International
400 Commonwealth Drive
Warrendale, PA 15096-0001
Tel: 877-606-7323
http://automobile.sae.org

For information on certification, contact
Society of Manufacturing Engineers
One SME Drive
Dearborn, MI 48121-2408
Tel: 800-733-4763
http://www.sme.org

———— INTERVIEW ————

Jerome Cortez is an engineering manager for front suspensions and axles at Hendrickson Truck Systems. He entered the automotive field right out of college 13 years ago. Jerome discussed the field with the editors of Careers in Focus: Automotives.

Q. What is one thing that young people may not know about a career in automotive engineering?

A. It may already be known, but automotive engineering is very diverse in subject and job responsibilities. For example, the product you work on can be individual components like suspensions, axles, transmissions, and engines, or a complete system of these components designing how they all work together. Within each component or subsystem, your job function may be as a project engineer who primarily coordinates the technical work of internal as well as external people to launch a product line, or as one of many functional engineers who does the technical work, such as finite element analysis (a computer simulation technique), lab testing, or vehicle testing.

You can also wear several hats and do some of everything. The number of hats you wear is usually in inverse proportion to the size of the company. The larger the company, the more compartmentalized the functions become; the smaller the company is, the more versatile an engineer needs to be since most small- to medium-sized companies can not justify the specialized functions.

Q. How did you train for this job?

A. On-the-job training was a key part of my training. My mentor was my supervisor and he put a lot of value on the technical aspect of engineering. Not all companies are able to invest in a formal training or mentoring program, and most are usually the larger companies and are able to invest the time and money to be able to train, then place, employees. Most medium to small companies hire to an immediate need for a position. This is why most mentoring relationships in these companies are formed informally while working together, like mine with my supervisor.

Another source of training was reference books. I had to refresh my memory on various topics using my college textbooks on my own time. I would recommend keeping all of your college textbooks. My college major was in mechanical engineering. I have also attended many seminars held by the Society of Automotive Engineers, the American Society of Mechanical Engineers, and other organizations.

Q. What are the most important personal and professional qualities for people in your career?

A. Contrary to popular belief, you actually need to be a people person to succeed in engineering. In almost all types of engineering, you have to deal with other people to get things done and your people skills can contribute to your success or can be your downfall. Another trait that most engineers have inherently is problem-solving skills. I am not sure if this is taught at school or those with this trait are drawn to engineering and it is reinforced. An engineer can typically learn to work across a myriad of fields because the one common thing all engineers do is solve problems.

Q. What is the future employment outlook for automotive engineers?

A. People will always need transportation. You need food and a home. The food, furniture, and materials need to get from where they are made or stored to you or your house, so the automotive and transportation industry is here to stay.

Unfortunately, the Big Three have taken a large blow in the past decade, and most recently Ford and Chrysler have seen major changes. The good news is that business is always changing and business models are always changing. I believe we have gone through some globalization of engineering and sourcing, and as an industry we are feeling the impact of that, both good and bad. We can not compete with the global labor market, so our strength in the future will be in our technical capabilities.

As a final note, the emerging market is Asia, namely China and India. Start taking those Mandarin classes because it will not be long until they become a technical superpower.

Automotive Industry Workers

OVERVIEW

Automotive industry workers are the people who work in the parts production and assembly plants of automobile manufacturers. Their labor involves work from the smallest part to the completed automobiles. Automotive industry workers read specifications; design parts; build, maintain, and operate machinery and tools used to produce parts; and assemble the automobiles.

HISTORY

In our mobile society, it is difficult to imagine a time without automobiles. Yet just over 100 years ago, there were none. In the late 1800s, inventors were just beginning to tinker with the idea of a self-propelled vehicle. Early experiments used steam to power a vehicle's engine. Two German engineers developed the first internal combustion engine fueled by gasoline. Karl Benz finished the first model in 1885, and Gottlieb Daimler finished building a similar model in 1886. Others around the world had similar successes in the late 1800s and early 1900s. In these early days, no one imagined people would become so reliant on the automobile as a way of life. In 1898, 50 automobile manufacturing companies were in operation in the United States, a number that rose to 241 by 1908.

Early automobiles were expensive to make and keep in working order and could be used to travel only short distances; they were "toys" for those who had the time and money to tinker with them. One such person was Henry Ford. He differed from others who had succeeded in building automobiles in that he believed the automobile could appeal to the general public if the cost of producing them were reduced. The Model A was first produced by the Ford Motor Company in small quantities in 1903. Ford made improvements to the Model A, and in October 1908, he found success with the more practical Model T—the vehicle that changed Ford's fortune and would eventually change the world. The Model T was a powerful car with a possible speed of 45 miles per hour that could run 13 to 21 miles on a gallon of gasoline. Such improvements were made possible by the use of vanadium steel, a lighter and more durable steel than that previously used. Automobiles were beginning to draw interest from the general public as newspapers reported early successes, but they were still out of reach for most Americans. The automobile remained a curiosity to be read about in the newspapers until 1913 when Ford changed the way his workers produced automobiles in the factory. Before 1913, skilled craftsmen made automobiles in Ford's factory, but Ford's moving assembly line reduced the skill level needed and sped up production. The moving assembly line improved the speed of chassis assembly from 12 hours and 8 minutes to 1 hour and 33 minutes. Craftsmen were no longer needed to make the parts and assemble the automobiles. Anyone could be trained for most of the jobs required to build an automobile in one of Ford's factories, making it possible to hire unskilled workers at lower wages.

For many early automotive workers, Ford's mass production concept proved to be both a blessing and a curse. Demand was growing for the affordable automobile, even during the Depression years, bringing new jobs for people who desperately needed them. However, working on an assembly line could be tedious and stressful at the same time. Ford paid his workers well (he introduced the $5 day in 1914, a high wage for the time), but he demanded a lot of them. He sped up the assembly line on several occasions, and many workers performed the same task for hours at a frenzied pace, often without a break.

Such conditions led workers to organize unions and, through the years, workers have gained more control over the speed at which they work and pay rates. Many of today's automotive industry workers belong to unions such as the United Auto Workers (founded in 1936). The industry continued to evolve with automotive technology in the 1940s and 1950s. American automobiles were generally large and consumed a lot of gasoline, but a strong U.S. economy afforded many Americans the ability to buy and maintain such vehicles. In Europe and Japan, smaller, fuel-efficient cars were more popular. This allowed foreign automakers to cut deeply into the American automobile market during fuel shortages in the 1970s. Automotive workers suffered job cuts in the 1980s because of declining exports and domestic sales. After rebounding in the early 2000s, the automotive industry is again facing challenging times as a result of strong competition from foreign automotive manufacturers and the outsourcing of vehicle and parts manufacturing to foreign countries where labor is less expensive and unions do not have as much strength. The United States currently has about one-quarter of the world's automobiles, some 147 million vehicles.

THE JOB

The term "automotive industry worker" covers the wide range of people who build the 7.5 million cars produced in the United States each year. Automotive industry workers are employed in two types of plants: parts production and assembly plants. Similar jobs are also found with companies that manufacture farm and earth-moving equipment; their workers often belong to the same unions and undergo the same training. Major automobile manufacturers are generally organized so that automobiles are assembled at a few large plants that employ several thousand workers. Parts for the automobiles are made at smaller plants that may employ fewer than 100 workers. Some plants that produce parts are not owned by the automobile manufacturer but may be independent companies that specialize in making one important part. These independent manufacturers may supply parts to several different automobile makers.

Whether they work in a parts plant or an assembly plant, automotive workers generally work with their hands; spend a lot of time standing, bending, and lifting; and do a lot of repetitive work. They often work in noisy areas and are required to wear protective equipment, such as safety glasses, earplugs, gloves, and masks, throughout their workday. Because automotive industry workers often work in large plants that operate 24 hours a day, they usually work in shifts. Shift assignments are generally made on the basis of seniority.

Precision metalworker is one of the more highly skilled positions found in automotive production plants. Precision metalworkers create the metal tools, dies, and special guiding and holding devices that produce automotive parts—thus, they are sometimes called *tool and die makers.* They must be familiar with the entire manufacturing process and have knowledge of mathematics, blueprint reading, and the properties of metals, such as hardness and heat tolerance. Precision metalworkers may perform all or some of the steps needed to make machining tools, including reading blueprints, planning the sequence of operations, marking the materials, and cutting and assembling the materials into a tool. Precision metalworkers often work in quieter parts of the production plants.

Precision machinists make the precision metal parts needed for automobiles using tools such as lathes, drill presses, and milling machines. In automotive production plants, their work is repetitive as they generally produce large quantities of one part. Machinists may spend their entire shift machining the part. Some machinists also read blueprints or written specifications for a part. They calculate where to cut into the metal, how fast to feed the metal into the machine, or how much of the metal to remove. Machinists select tools and materials needed for the job and mark the metal stock for the cuts to be made. Increasingly, the machine tools used to make automotive parts are computerized. Computer numerically controlled machining is widespread in many manufacturing processes today. *Tool programmers* write the computer programs that direct the machine's operations, and machinists monitor the computer-controlled process.

Maintenance workers is a general category that refers to a number of jobs. Maintenance workers may repair or make new parts for existing machines. They also may set up new machines. They may work with sales representatives from the company that sold the automobile manufacturer the piece of equipment. Maintenance workers are responsible for the upkeep of machines and should be able to perform all of the machine's operations.

Welders use equipment that joins metal parts by melting and fusing them to form a permanent bond. There are different types of welds as well as equipment to make the welds. In manual welding, the work is controlled entirely by the welder. Other work is semi-automatic, in which machinery such as a wire feeder is used to help perform the weld. Much of the welding work in automotive plants is repetitive; in some of these cases, *welding machine operators* monitor machines as they perform the welding tasks. Because they work with fire, welders must wear safety gear, such as protective clothing, safety shoes, goggles, and hoods with protective lenses.

Inspectors check the manufacturing process at all stages to make sure products meet quality standards. Everything from raw materials to parts to the finished automobile is checked for dimensions, color, weight, texture, strength, and other physical characteristics, as well as proper operation. Inspectors identify and record any quality problems and may work with any of several departments to remedy the flaw. Jobs for inspectors are declining because inspection has become automated at many stages of production. Also, there is a move to have workers self-check their work on the production line.

Floor or line supervisors are responsible for a group of workers who produce one part or perform one step in a process. They may report to department heads or foremen who oversee several such departments. Many supervisors are production workers who have worked their way up the ranks; still others have a management background and, in many cases, a college degree in business or management.

REQUIREMENTS

High School
Many automotive industry jobs require mechanical skills, so you should take advantage of any shop programs your high school offers, such as auto mechanics, electronics, welding, drafting, and computer programming and design. In the core subject areas, mathematics, including algebra and geometry, is useful for reading blueprints and computer programs that direct machine functions. Chemistry is useful for workers who need to be familiar with the properties of metals. English classes are also important to help you communicate verbally with both supervisors and coworkers and to read and understand complex instructions.

Postsecondary Training
Many of the jobs in an automotive plant are classified as semiskilled or unskilled positions, and people with some mechanical aptitude, physical ability, and a high school diploma are qualified to do them. However, there is often stiff competition for jobs with large automakers like General Motors, Ford, and Chrysler LLC because they offer good benefits and pay compared to jobs that require similar skill levels. Therefore, if you have some postsecondary training, certification, or experience, you stand a better chance of getting a job in the automotive industry than someone with only a high school diploma.

Formal training for machining, welding, and toolmaking is offered at vocational schools, vocational-technical institutes, community colleges, and private schools. Increasingly, such postsecondary training or certification is the route many workers take to getting an automotive industry job. In the past, apprenticeships and on-the-job training were the paths many workers took to get factory jobs, but these options are not as widely available today. Electricians, who generally must complete an apprenticeship, may find work in automotive plants as maintenance workers.

Certification or Licensing

Certification is available but not required for many of the positions in an automotive production plant. The American Welding Society offers the designations certified welding engineer, certified associate welding inspector, and certified welding inspector to members who meet education and professional experience criteria as well as pass an examination. For precision metalworkers and machinists, the National Tooling and Machining Association operates training centers and apprentice programs and sets skill standards.

Other Requirements

Working in an automotive production plant can be physically challenging. For many jobs, you need the physical capability to stand for long periods, lift heavy objects, and maneuver hand tools and machinery. Of course, some jobs in an automotive production plant can be performed by a person with a physical disability. For example, a person who uses a wheelchair may work well on an assembly line job that requires only the use of his or her hands. Automotive workers should have hand and finger dexterity and the ability to do repetitive work accurately and safely.

EXPLORING

Do you enjoy working with your hands? Following complex instructions? Do you think you could do repetitive work on a daily basis? Are you a natural leader who would enjoy a supervisory position? Once you have an idea what area of the automotive industry you want to pursue, the best way to learn more is to find someone who does the job and ask him or her questions about the work. Assembly plants are generally located in or near large cities, but if you live in a rural area, you can still probably find someone with a similar job at a parts plant or other manufacturer. Even small towns generally have machine shops or other types of manufacturing plants that employ machinists, tool and die makers, inspectors, and other production workers. Local machine shops or factories are good places to get experience, perhaps through a summer or after-school job to see if you enjoy working in a production environment. Many high schools have cooperative programs that employ students who want to gain work experience.

EMPLOYERS

Automotive industry workers can find jobs with domestic automakers, such as the Big Three, and with foreign automakers like Mitsubishi and Honda, which both have large assembly plants in the United States. Large assembly plants may employ several thousand workers. Parts production plants may employ fewer workers, but there are more of these plants. Assembly plants are generally located in or near large cities, especially in the Northeast and Midwest where heavy manufacturing is concentrated. Parts production plants vary in size, from a few dozen workers to several hundred. Employees of these plants may all work on one small part or on several parts that make up one component of an automobile. Parts production plants are located in smaller towns as well as urban areas. The production processes in agricultural and earth-moving equipment factories are similar to those in the automotive industry, and workers trained in welding, toolmaking, machining, and maintenance may find jobs with companies like Caterpillar and John Deere.

The United Auto Workers, the largest union in the industry, currently reports 640,000 active members.

STARTING OUT

Hiring practices at large plants are usually very structured. Such large employers generally don't place "help wanted" ads. Rather, they accept applications year-round and keep them on file. Applicants generally complete an initial application and may be placed on a hiring list. Others get started by working as temporary or part-time workers at the plant and using their experience and contacts to obtain full-time, permanent positions. Some plants work with career placement offices of vocational schools and technical associations to find qualified workers. Others may recruit workers at job fairs. Also, as with many large factories, people who have a relative or know someone who works at the plant usually have a better chance of getting hired. Their contact may put in a good word with a supervisor or advise them when an opening occurs.

New hires are usually expected to join the UAW (United Auto Workers) or another union. Unions help negotiate with manufacturers and deal with the company on a worker's behalf; however, they are also very structured.

ADVANCEMENT

Automotive production plants are very controlled in their paths of advancement. Large human resources departments oversee the personnel structures of all departments; each job has a specific description with specific qualifications. Union rules and contracts further impact advancement. Longevity is usually the key to advancement in an automotive plant. For many, advancement means staying in the same position and moving up on the salary scale. Others acquire experience and, often, further training to advance to a position with a higher skill level, more responsibility, and higher pay. For example, precision machinists may learn a lot about many different machines throughout their careers and may undergo training or be promoted to become precision metalworkers. Others with years of experience become supervisors of their departments.

EARNINGS

Salaries vary widely for automotive industry workers depending on their job and how long they've been with the company. Supervisors may earn $60,000 to $75,000 a year or more, depending on the number of people they supervise. Pay for semiskilled or unskilled workers, such as assemblers, is considerably lower, usually in the $30,000 to $40,000 range. Still, such production jobs are sought after because this pay is higher than such workers may find elsewhere based on their skill level. The *Career Guide to Industries* reports the following 2006 median annual earnings for workers in motor vehicle manufacturing: first-line managers, $64,438; inspectors, $52,936; team assemblers, $44,928; welders, $42,890. Those employed by motor vehicle parts manufacturers earned lower salaries. First-line managers earned median annual salaries of $48,922; machinists, $38,000; inspectors, $34,819; welders, $31,491; and team assemblers, $27,165.

Earnings are usually much higher for workers who are members of a union and employed by a Big Three automaker. Few of these workers earn less than $40,000 a year, and some earn as much as $100,000 a year because of mandatory overtime and six- or seven-day workweeks.

Workers employed by large, unionized companies such as Ford and Chrysler LLC enjoy good benefits, including paid health insurance and paid holidays, sick days, and personal days. Large employers generally offer retirement plans and many match workers' contributions to retirement funds. Automotive industry workers who work for independent parts manufacturers may not enjoy the comprehensive benefit programs that employees of large companies do, but generally are offered health insurance and paid personal days.

WORK ENVIRONMENT

Working as a production worker in an automotive plant can be stressful, depending on the worker's personality, job duties, and management expectations. Assembly line workers have little control over the speed at which they must complete their work. They can generally take breaks only when scheduled. Norm Ritchie, a machine operator at a Chrysler parts plant in Perrysburg, Ohio, says the job can be stressful: "The pressure [of the assembly line] affects people in different ways. Sometimes people get pretty stressed out; other people can handle it." Ritchie, who works on steering shafts, also said that noise is a concern in his area of the plant. He estimated that the noise level is about 90 decibels all the time. Automotive production workers must follow several safety precautions every day, including wearing protective gear (such as earplugs) and undergoing safety training throughout their careers.

OUTLOOK

The U.S. Department of Labor predicts that employment in motor vehicle and parts manufacturing will decline by 14 percent through 2016. The slowing economy could cause production slowdowns and subsequent layoffs for auto industry workers, particularly those who work for American manufacturers. Many manufacturers have also found it more cost effective to move operations overseas, where unions are weak and labor is cheaper. Additionally, high-technology production techniques have made workers more productive and reduced the number of workers needed for some manufacturing processes.

Despite this prediction, openings are expected as many automotive industry workers reach retirement age in the next several years. Additionally, the decline in employment among American-owned automakers has been balanced somewhat by new foreign-owned manufacturing plants that have been built in the United States. Today, many U.S. automotive workers are employed by foreign-owned automakers such as Honda and Mitsubishi. As of 2006, approximately 1.1 million workers were employed in the industry, according to the U.S. Bureau of Labor Statistics, still making it one of the largest manufacturing industries.

Workers with two-year degrees and a wide range of skills, such as in hydraulics, electrical systems, and welding, will have the best employment prospects.

FOR MORE INFORMATION

These professional societies promote the skills of their trades and can provide career information.

American Welding Society
550 Lejeune Road, NW
Miami, FL 33126-5699
Tel: 800-443-9353
Email: info@aws.org
http://www.aws.org

National Tooling and Machining Association
9300 Livingston Road
Fort Washington, MD 20744-4914
Tel: 800-248-6862
Email: info@ntma.org
http://www.ntma.org

For industry information, contact

Association of International Automobile Manufacturers
2111 Wilson Boulevard, Suite 1150
Arlington, VA 22201-3098
Tel: 703-525-7788
http://www.aiam.org

These are two of many unions that represent automotive production workers. They can provide information about training and education programs in your area.

International Association of Machinists and Aerospace Workers
9000 Machinists Place
Upper Marlboro, MD 20772-2687
Tel: 301-967-4500
http://www.iamaw.org

United Auto Workers
8000 East Jefferson Avenue
Detroit, MI 48214-3963
Tel: 313-926-5000
http://www.uaw.org

Diesel Mechanics

QUICK FACTS

School Subjects
Computer science
Technical/shop

Personal Skills
Following instructions
Mechanical/manipulative

Work Environment
Primarily indoors
Primarily one location

Minimum Education Level
High school diploma

Salary Range
$24,370 to $45,000 to
$55,890+

Certification or Licensing
Recommended

Outlook
About as fast as the average

DOT
625

GOE
05.03.01

NOC
7335

O*NET-SOC
49-3031.00

OVERVIEW

Diesel mechanics repair and maintain diesel engines that power trucks, buses, ships, construction and roadbuilding equipment, farm equipment, and some automobiles. They may also maintain and repair nonengine components, such as brakes, electrical systems, and heating and air-conditioning units. Approximately 275,000 diesel mechanics work in the United States.

HISTORY

In 1892, Rudolf Diesel patented an engine that, despite its weight and large size, was more efficient than the gasoline engine patented by Gottlieb Daimler less than a decade earlier. While Daimler's engine became the standard for automobiles, Diesel found his engine had practical use for industry. The diesel engine differs from the gasoline engine in that the ignition of fuel is caused by compression of air in the engine's cylinders rather than by a spark. Diesel's engines were eventually used to power pipelines, electric and water plants, automobiles and trucks, and marine craft. Equipment used in mines, oil fields, factories, and transoceanic shipping also came to rely on diesel engines. With the onset of World War I, diesel engines became standard in submarines, tanks, and other heavy equipment. Suddenly, diesel mechanics were in big demand and the armed forces established training programs. Combat units supported by diesel-powered machines often had several men trained in diesel mechanics to repair breakdowns. The war proved to the industry that diesel engines were tough and efficient, and many companies found applications for diesel-powered machines in the following years.

At the turn of the century, trucks were wooden wagons equipped with gasoline engines. As they became bigger, transported more goods, and traveled farther, fuel efficiency became a big concern. In 1930, the trucking industry adopted the diesel engine, with its efficiency and durability, as its engine for the future. Many diesel mechanics began their training as automobile mechanics, and learned diesel through hands-on experience. World War II brought a new demand for highly trained diesel mechanics, and again the armed forces trained men in diesel technology. After the war, diesel mechanics found new jobs in diesel at trucking companies that maintained large fleets of trucks, and at construction companies that used diesel-powered equipment. It wasn't until the 1970s that diesel engines in consumer passenger cars began to gain popularity. Before then, the disadvantages of diesel—its heaviness, poor performance, and low driving comfort—made diesel a second choice for many consumers. But the fuel crisis of the 1970s brought diesel a greater share of the automotive market, creating more demand for mechanics who could repair and maintain diesel engines.

Today, job growth and security for diesel mechanics is closely tied to the trucking industry. In the 1980s and 1990s, the trucking industry experienced steady growth as other means of transportation, such as rail, were used less frequently. Now, many businesses and manufacturers have found it cost efficient to maintain less inventory. Instead, they prefer to have their materials shipped on an as-needed basis. This low-inventory system has created a tremendous demand on the trucking industry, and diesel mechanics are essential to helping the industry meet that demand.

THE JOB

Most diesel mechanics work on the engines of heavy trucks, such as those used in hauling freight over long distances, or in heavy industries such as construction and mining. Many are employed by companies that maintain their own fleet of vehicles. The diesel mechanic's main task is preventive maintenance to avoid breakdowns, but they also make engine repairs when necessary. Diesel mechanics also frequently perform maintenance on other nonengine components, such as brake systems, electronics, transmissions, and suspensions.

Through periodic maintenance, diesel mechanics keep vehicles and engines in good operating condition. They run through a checklist of standard maintenance tasks, such as changing oil and filters, checking cooling systems, and inspecting brakes and wheel bearings for wear. They make the appropriate repairs or adjustments and replace parts that are worn. Fuel injection units, fuel pumps, pistons, crankshafts, bushings, and bearings must be regularly removed, reconditioned, or replaced.

As more diesel engines rely on a variety of electronic components, mechanics have become more proficient in the basics of electronics. Previously technical functions in diesel equipment (both engine and nonengine parts) are being replaced by electronics, significantly altering the way mechanics perform maintenance and repairs. As new technology evolves, diesel mechanics may need additional training to use tools and computers to diagnose and correct problems with electronic parts. Employers generally provide this training.

Diesel engines are scheduled for periodic rebuilding usually every 18 months or 100,000 miles. Mechanics rely upon extensive records they keep on each engine to determine the extent of the rebuild. Records detail the maintenance and repair history that helps mechanics determine repair needs and prevent future breakdowns. Diesel mechanics use various specialty instruments to make precision measurements and diagnostics of each engine component. Micrometers and various gauges test for engine wear. Ohmmeters, ammeters, and voltmeters test electrical components. Dynamometers and oscilloscopes test overall engine operations.

Engine rebuilds usually require several mechanics, each specializing in a particular area. They use ordinary hand tools such as ratchets and sockets, screwdrivers, wrenches, and pliers; power tools such as pneumatic wrenches; welding and flame-cutting equipment; and machine tools like lathes and boring machines. Diesel mechanics typically supply their own hand tools at an investment of $6,000 to $25,000, depending upon their specialty. It is the employer's responsibility to furnish the larger power tools, engine analyzers, and other diagnostic equipment.

In addition to trucks and buses, diesel mechanics also service and repair construction equipment such as cranes, bulldozers, earth moving equipment, and road construction equipment. The variations in transmissions, gear systems, electronics, and other engine components of diesel engines may require additional training.

To maintain and increase their skills and to keep up with new technology, diesel mechanics must regularly read service and repair manuals, industry bulletins, and other publications. They must also be willing to take part in training programs given by manufacturers or at vocational schools. Those who have certification must periodically retake exams to keep their credentials. Frequent changes in technology demand that mechanics keep up-to-date with the latest training.

REQUIREMENTS

High School

A high school diploma is the minimum requirement to land a job that offers growth possibilities, a good salary, and challenges. In addition to automotive and shop classes, high school students should take mathematics, English, and computer classes. Adjustments and repairs to many car components require the mechanic to make numerous computations, for which good mathematical skills will be essential. Diesel mechanics must be voracious readers to stay competitive; there are many must-read repair manuals and trade journals. Computer skills are also important, as computers are common in most repair shops.

Postsecondary Training

Employers prefer to hire those who have completed some kind of formal training program in diesel mechanics, or in some cases automobile mechanics—usually a minimum of two years' education in either case. A wide variety of such programs are offered by community colleges, vocational schools, independent organizations, and manufacturers. Most accredited programs include periods of internship.

Some programs are conducted in association with truck and heavy equipment manufacturers. Students combine work experience with hands-on classroom study of up-to-date equipment provided by manufacturers. In other programs students alternate time in the classroom with internships at manufacturers. Although these students may take up to four years to finish their training, they become familiar with the latest technology and also earn modest salaries as they train.

Certification or Licensing

One indicator of quality for entry-level mechanics recognized by everyone in the industry is certification by the National Institute for Automotive Service Excellence. There are eight areas of certification available in medium/heavy-duty truck repair: gasoline engines; diesel engines; drivetrain; brakes; suspension and steering; electrical/electronic systems; heating, ventilation, and air conditioning; and preventive maintenance inspection. There are seven areas of certification available in school bus repair: body systems and special equipment, diesel engines, drivetrain, brakes, suspension and steering, electrical/electronic systems, and air-conditioning systems and controls. Applicants must have at least two years of experience in the field and pass the examinations related to their specialty. To maintain their certification, mechanics must retake the examination

A mechanic repairs a diesel engine. *(David Frazier, The Image Works)*

for their specialties every five years. The Association of Diesel Specialists also offers voluntary certification to diesel mechanics.

Other Requirements
Diesel mechanics must be patient and thorough in their work. They need to have excellent troubleshooting skills and must be able to logically deduce the cause of system malfunctions. Diesel mechanics also need a Class A driver's license.

EXPLORING

Many community centers offer general auto maintenance workshops where students can get additional practice working on real cars and learn from instructors. Trade magazines such as *Land Line* (http://www.landlinemag.com) and *Overdrive* (http://www.overdriveonline.com) are excellent sources for learning what's new in the trucking industry and can be found at libraries and some larger bookstores. Working part time at a repair shop or dealership can prepare students for the atmosphere and challenges a mechanic faces on the job.

Many diesel mechanics begin their exploration on gasoline engines because spare diesel engines are hard to come by for those who are just trying to learn and experiment. Diesel engines are very similar to gasoline engines except for their ignition systems and size. Besides being larger, diesel engines are distinguished by the absence of common gasoline engine components such as spark plugs, ignition wires, coils, and distributors. Diesel mechanics use the same hand tools as automobile mechanics, however, and in this way learning technical aptitude on automobiles will be important for the student who wishes to eventually learn to work on diesel engines.

EMPLOYERS

Diesel mechanics may find employment in a number of different areas. Many work for dealers that sell semitrucks and other diesel-powered equipment. About 17 percent of the country's 275,000 diesel mechanics work for local and long-distance trucking companies. Others maintain the buses and trucks of public transit companies, schools, or governments or service buses, trucks, and other diesel-powered equipment at automotive repair and maintenance shops, motor vehicle and parts wholesalers, or automotive equipment rental and leasing agencies. Diesel mechanics can find work all over the country, in both large and small cities. Job titles may range from bus maintenance technician to hydraulic system technician, clutch rebuilder, and heavy-duty maintenance mechanic. A small number of diesel mechanics may find jobs in the railway and industrial sectors and in marine maintenance.

STARTING OUT

The best way to begin a career as a diesel mechanic is to enroll in a postsecondary training program and obtain accreditation. Trade and technical schools nearly always provide job placement assistance for their graduates. Such schools usually have contacts with local employers who need to hire well-trained people. Often, employers post job openings at accredited trade schools in their area.

Although postsecondary training programs are more widely available and popular today, some mechanics still learn the trade on the job as apprentices. Their training consists of working for several years under the guidance of experienced mechanics. Trainees usually begin as helpers, lubrication workers, or service station attendants, and gradually acquire the skills and knowledge necessary for many service or repair tasks. However, fewer employers today are willing to hire apprentices because of the time and cost it takes to train them. Those who do learn their skills on the job inevitably require some formal training if they wish to advance and stay in step with the changing industry.

Intern programs sponsored by truck manufacturers or independent organizations provide students with opportunities to actually work with prospective employers. Internships can provide students with valuable contacts who will be able to recommend future employers once students have completed their classroom training. Many students may even be hired by the company for which they interned.

ADVANCEMENT

Typically the first step a mechanic must take to advance is to receive certification. Although certification is voluntary, it is a widely recognized standard of achievement for diesel mechanics and the way many advance. The more certification a mechanic has, the more his or her worth to an employer, and the higher he or she advances.

With today's complex diesel engine and truck components requiring hundreds of hours of study and practice to master, more employers prefer to hire certified mechanics. Certification assures the employer that the employee is skilled in the latest repair procedures and is familiar with the most current diesel technology. Those with good communication and planning skills may advance to shop supervisor or service manager at larger repair shops or companies that keep large fleets. Others with good business skills go into business for themselves and open their own shops or work as freelance mechanics. Some master mechanics may teach at technical and vocational schools or at community colleges.

EARNINGS

Diesel mechanics' earnings vary depending upon their region, industry (trucking, construction, railroad), and other factors. According to the U.S. Department of Labor, the median hourly pay for all diesel mechanics in 2006 was $18.11, or approximately $37,660 annually, for full-time employment; the lowest paid 10 percent of diesel mechanics earned approximately $11.71 an hour, or $24,370 a year, while the highest paid 10 percent earned more than $26.50 an hour, amounting to $55,120 a year. Mechanics who work for companies that must operate around the clock, such as bus lines, may work at night, on weekends, or on holidays and receive extra pay for this work.

The highest paid diesel mechanics work in motor vehicle manufacturing. They earned a mean hourly wage of $26.87 an hour, or $55,890 a year, in 2006. Those who worked for general freight trucking companies earned a mean hourly wage of $17.19, or $35,760 a year, and those who specialized in automotive repair and maintenance earned an average of $17.79 an hour, or $37,000 a year.

Many diesel mechanics are members of labor unions, and their wage rates are established by contracts between the union and the employer. Benefits packages vary from business to business. Mechanics can expect health insurance and paid vacation from most employers. Other benefits may include dental and eye care, life and disability insurance, and a pension plan. Employers usually cover a mechanic's work clothes through a clothing allowance and may pay a percentage of hand tools purchases. An increasing number of employers pay all or most of an employee's certification training if he or she passes the test. A mechanic's salary can increase by yearly bonuses or profit sharing if the business does well.

WORK ENVIRONMENT

Depending on the size of the shop and whether it is a trucking or construction company, government, or private business, diesel mechanics work with anywhere from two to 20 other mechanics. Most shops are well lighted and well ventilated. They can be frequently noisy due to running trucks and equipment. Hoses are attached to exhaust pipes and led outside to avoid carbon monoxide poisoning.

Minor hand and back injuries are the most common problem for diesel mechanics. When reaching in hard-to-get-at places or loosening tight bolts, mechanics often bruise, cut, or burn their hands. With caution and experience most mechanics learn to avoid hand injuries. Working for long periods of time in cramped or bent positions often results in a stiff back or neck. Diesel mechanics also lift many heavy objects that can cause injury if not handled cautiously; however, most shops have small cranes or hoists to lift the heaviest objects. Some may experience allergic reactions to the variety of solvents and oils frequently used in cleaning, maintenance, and repair. Shops must comply with strict safety procedures to help employees avoid accidents. Most mechanics work between 40- and 50-hour workweeks, but may be required to work longer hours when the shop is busy or during emergencies. Some mechanics make emergency repairs to stranded, roadside trucks or to construction equipment.

OUTLOOK

With diesel technology getting better (smaller, smarter, and less noisy), more light trucks, buses, and other vehicles (including some automobiles) and equipment are switching to diesel engines. Diesel engines are already more fuel efficient than gasoline engines. Also, the increased reliance by businesses for quick deliveries has increased the demand on trucking companies. Many businesses maintain lower inventories of materials, instead preferring to have items shipped more frequently. The increase in diesel-powered vehicles, together with a trend toward increased cargo transportation via trucks, will create jobs for highly skilled diesel mechanics. Less skilled workers will face tough competition. The U.S. Department of Labor predicts that employment will grow about as fast as the average for all occupations through 2016.

Diesel mechanics enjoy good job security. Fluctuations in the economy have little effect on employment in this field. When the economy is bad, people service and repair their trucks and equipment rather than replace them. Conversely, when the economy is good more people are apt to service their trucks and equipment regularly as well as buy new trucks and equipment.

The most jobs for diesel mechanics will open up at trucking companies who hire mechanics to maintain and repair their fleets. Construction companies are also expected to require an increase in diesel mechanics to maintain their heavy machinery, such as cranes, earthmovers, and other diesel-powered equipment.

FOR MORE INFORMATION

For information on certification, contact
Association of Diesel Specialists
10 Laboratory Drive
PO Box 13966
Research Triangle Park, NC 27709-3966
Tel: 919-406-8804
Email: info@diesel.org
http://www.diesel.org

For information on the automotive service industry and continuing education programs, contact
Automotive Aftermarket Industry Association
7101 Wisconsin Avenue, Suite 1300
Bethesda, MD 20814-3415

Tel: 301-654-6664
Email: aaia@aftermarket.org
http://www.aftermarket.org

For information on training, accreditation, and testing, contact
I-CAR
5125 Trillium Boulevard
Hoffman Estates, IL 60192-3600
Tel: 800-422-7872
http://www.i-car.com

For career information and information on certified programs,
contact
National Automotive Technicians Education Foundation
101 Blue Seal Drive, Suite 101
Leesburg, VA 20175-5646
Tel: 703-669-6650
http://www.natef.org

For information on becoming a certified mechanic, contact
National Institute for Automotive Service Excellence
101 Blue Seal Drive, Suite 101
Leesburg, VA 20175-5646
Tel: 888-ASE-TEST
http://www.asecert.org

For information on careers, visit
Automotive Careers Today
http://www.autocareerstoday.net

INTERVIEW

Rick Burnett is the coordinator of the Diesel Technology Program
at Ashland Community and Technical College (http://www.ash-
land.kctcs.edu) in Ashland, Kentucky. He discussed the field with
the editors of Careers in Focus: Automotives.

Q. Please tell us about your program and your background.

A. The program is certified by the National Automotive Technicians Education Foundation/National Institute for Automotive
Service Excellence (ASE). It is a two-year program including a
10-credit summer term depending on the path taken. We offer
two associate of applied science/general occupational technical
studies degrees—one in construction equipment technology

and the other in medium/heavy truck technician. We also offer diplomas in these areas and in farm machinery technician along with 12 certificates. The program covers all aspects of repair (powertrain, engines, antilock brake systems (ABS), electrical, steering and suspension, hydraulics, preventive maintenance, and troubleshooting). There are two instructors in our program. I am an ASE master certified auto and medium/heavy truck technician, but my main background is construction equipment as I worked on strip mining for about 14 years and have been teaching about 21 years. The other instructor, Shannon McCarty, has about 14 years of experience with trucks and construction equipment and has his certification in medium/heavy truck.

Q. What is one thing that young people may not know about a career in diesel technology?

A. This can be a very rewarding career. We often see technicians making in excess of $100,000. We have moved into the computer age where everything on the trucks and equipment is computer controlled (i.e., engine controls, ABS brakes, load-sensing steering, and transmission controls). There is a shortage of trained technicians, and it is only getting worse. Large shops are recruiting electricians, automotive technicians, and others to try to keep up with the need for technicians.

Q. What types of students pursue study in your program?

A. Most of the students who do well in this career are those who like to work with their hands. They need to have good math skills and be able to read for information and comprehend the material to repair today's equipment. We get a lot of students from agriculture, welding, and automotive programs.

Q. What advice would you offer diesel technology majors as they graduate and look for jobs?

A. The construction equipment field pays better than the truck field, but you can make good money in either. Students need to do what they like and not worry as much about the money. There are plenty of opportunities in either field.

Q. What is the employment outlook in the field?

A. There is a shortage of technicians and a lot more are close to retirement age. Anyone willing to work in this field can make a good living with some job security. The shops around here are stealing the better techs by offering better money so it looks good for the younger people coming into the market.

Driving School Owners and Instructors

OVERVIEW

Driving instructors, also known as *driving safety educators*, teach people the rules of the road and skills needed to drive safely. Their teaching methods include classroom lectures covering driving theory, traffic rules and laws, and automobile maintenance, as well monitoring students as they drive a car. Some instructors specialize by type of vehicle (such as cars, trucks, buses, or motorcycles).

HISTORY

The need for instructors to teach people how to drive has existed for as long as there have been cars on the road. But it was not until the 1930s that formal driver education courses were created. Early traffic safety lessons were incorporated with general safety classes or taught as a separate class in a classroom setting (with no actual on-the-road training).

In 1932, Amos Neyhart, a professor at Pennsylvania State College High School, taught the first driving instruction course that included both classroom and behind-the-wheel modules. By 1940, more than 20 states offered driving instruction courses, and several hundred high schools began teaching driver education.

In 1947, 200,000 students were enrolled in driver education programs at 3,000 public high schools across the United States, according to "Teen Driver Education," by Dr. Richard Compton of the National Highway Traffic Safety Administration (NHTSA). By

School Subjects
Business
Speech

Personal Skills
Leadership/management
Helping/teaching

Work Environment
Indoors and outdoors
Primarily multiple locations

Minimum Education Level
Some postsecondary training

Salary Range
$20,800 to $47,740 to $76,100+

Certification or Licensing
Required by certain states

Outlook
About as fast as the average

DOT
099

GOE
N/A

NOC
4216

O*NET-SOC
25-3021.00

1976, the number had increased to 3.2 million students at 17,000 public high schools.

In the late 1970s and early 1980s, the number of students taking driver education classes at public schools declined due to questions regarding its effectiveness and its removal from a list of priority programs by the NHTSA. This decline created many opportunities for private driving instructors, and many new driving instruction schools opened in the following decades.

Today, driving schools and programs at public high schools continue to help people became safe and decisive drivers.

The American Driver and Traffic Safety Education Association offers professional guidance and continuing education to many driving instructors. The National Driving Instructors Institute, another professional association, keeps members informed of new methods and techniques of driving instruction.

THE JOB

Driving instructors teach students the rules of the road and the proper and safe way to drive. Instructors can teach driver education at public high schools or through private driving schools. Instructors in public schools are often certified to teach driver education, but may also teach other subjects as well. Some instructors may be contracted by schools to teach driver education. Private driving schools employ instructors on a full- or part-time basis

Driver education is taught in two sections: classroom instruction and practical instruction. Topics covered in classroom lectures include rules of the road, signs and signals, traffic regulations, and basic operation of the car. Instructors also teach driver rights versus pedestrian rights, proper steps to take during road emergencies, driving techniques during inclement weather, and defensive driving. Time may also be spent teaching students how to change a flat tire, or how to mark a disabled car. Another important topic covered during classroom time is the danger of driving under the influence of drugs or alcohol. In recent times, instructors have also addressed the hazards of other driving distractions such as cell phones, text messaging, or using headphones while driving. Instructors use a combination of lectures, movies or slide shows, class discussion, and projects to educate students. Some projects may include clipping current newspaper articles regarding automobile accidents and discussing each particular situation and how to avoid them in the future. Some high schools may also present live presentations demonstrating the tragedies of unsafe driving, including staged productions of multicar accidents.

Once students are given a learner's permit, they are ready for practical experience behind the wheel. Some schools have auto simulators that allow students to test their driving skills without actually leaving the classroom. Such programs help students hone their techniques by navigating their "car" in traffic, making turns, and parking.

When students are ready to tackle the road, instructors rely on specially designed cars that have dual steering wheels and rearview mirrors, and brakes located on both the driver's and instructor's sides. Instructors teach students how to start the car, check for oncoming traffic, and navigate safely onto the road. Students are also able to practice braking smoothly to a stop, making turns, and navigating through traffic. Other skills, such as parallel parking, merging onto traffic, and putting the car in reverse, are practiced until the students become comfortable with these tasks. Students practice driving on various types of roads such as city streets, highways, and on rural roads to get a feel for different levels of traffic and speed. The instructor can also gauge the comfort level of students as they drive, and is able to use his or her own set of controls in case of emergencies. Other students often ride as passengers, and take turns behind the wheel.

Once all requirements of driver education are met, and students are comfortable behind the wheel of a car, instructors may suggest they take the state test to qualify for a driver's license. The duration of driver education varies according to the school. In public school, driver education can last one quarter to a semester during the school year or six weeks in the summer. Classes taught at private driving schools usually last anywhere from four weeks to two months.

Some driving instructors specialize in a type of vehicle, such as a commercial truck or motorcycle. They often teach individuals the skills needed to operate these vehicles for work purposes, such as driving a bus or semitruck. Such instructors must be certified and approved according to the specifications of their state's department of motor vehicles. Commercial driving instructors are contracted or employed by commercial driving schools.

REQUIREMENTS

High School

A few classes can help prepare you for a career in driving instruction. You should do well in your own driver education classes, as knowledge of the rules of the road and familiarity of the maintenance and operation of a car is imperative. Communications and speech classes

A driving instructor (left) gives a student directions during a driver education class. *(Seth Perlman, Associated Press)*

are also important since instructors must be able to convey ideas and techniques to their students.

Postsecondary Training

A college degree is not necessary except at certain high schools where driver education is taught by licensed teachers. In such cases, a degree in education, or comparable major, is required. If you aspire to operate your own driving school, you may want to consider taking college-level business courses. Classes such as accounting, marketing, or business management will help you set up a successful operation.

Certification and Licensing

A valid driver's license is a prerequisite for employment in this field, as well as a clean driving record.

Licensure requirements vary from state to state. In Massachusetts, for example, all driving schools and their instructors must be registered with the state's Registry of Motor Vehicles. Check with your state motor vehicle department for required documents.

Other Requirements

A desire to teach and help others is an important quality for driving instructors. They also need to be patient and level-headed in case students become nervous or panic when encountering different driving situations. Instructors are experts in the rules of the road, as well as basic car maintenance. It is also imperative to have a good driving record. Some schools may conduct a background check before employment.

Driving school owners should be organized, detail-minded, and have strong business skills.

EXPLORING

To learn more about this career, try contacting a local driving school. You can interview instructors to learn what skills are needed to teach students of all ages and abilities. By spending time with the school's owner, you can see firsthand what it takes to register students, make employee schedules, maintain a fleet of cars, and other tasks needed to run a business.

During your driver education classes, pay attention to the teaching techniques of your own instructor. Does he or she rely mostly on classroom lectures or bring in other sources or projects to spur interest and discussion? Ask yourself what you would do to add creativity when teaching this important topic. You can also ask your instructor to participate in an information interview about his or her career.

EMPLOYERS

Driving instructors are employed by public high schools and private driving schools. Opportunities are available throughout the United States, but best in areas that have a large population.

STARTING OUT

As a new instructor, you may be scheduled to assist more experienced instructors before being given your own roster of students. With time and training, you may be given more teaching responsibility, both in the classroom and on the road.

ADVANCEMENT

With experience, instructors can advance from teaching high school-level driver education to teaching at other facilities such as state-run driving schools or driving facilities. Some instructors choose to teach a specialized group of students such as the elderly or disabled. Other instructors choose to teach driving techniques for other vehicles including commercial trucks, motorcycles, and race cars.

Some driving instructors may open their own schools. As proprietor, they may hire other instructors to handle class instruction, leaving their time free for the day-to-day tasks of operating a business.

EARNINGS

The U.S. Department of Labor does not offer salary information for the career of driving school owner or instructor. According to limited information, driving instructors earn hourly salaries of approximately $10 to $20 an hour. Driving instructors at public high schools who work as salaried educators have the same earnings as regular teachers. According to the U.S. Department of Labor, the median annual salary for secondary school teachers was $47,740 in 2006. The lowest 10 percent earned less than $31,760; the highest 10 percent earned $76,100 or more.

Driving instructors who work for a company usually receive benefits such as sick leave, health and life insurance, vacation days, and a savings and pension program. Driving school owners must provide their own benefits.

WORK ENVIRONMENT

Driving instructors work both indoors and outdoors. They give lectures and monitor simulation time inside a classroom. They also spend a great deal of time teaching from behind the wheel of an automobile, in a variety of driving situations ranging from side streets to busy highways.

While both private and public instructors work year-round, their hours vary significantly. Those teaching in public schools do so within the hours of a regular school day and week. Some instructors may also have other teaching duties aside from driver's education. Instructors employed at a private driving school have more flexible hours—including evening hours and weekends. Summer months are especially busy as some students choose to tackle driver education separate from their regular school curriculum.

While public and private driving instructors are responsible for teaching groups of students, commercial driving instructors often teach students one on one.

OUTLOOK

Employment opportunities should continue to be strong for driving school owners and instructors. Students will continue to enroll in driver's education, either through their public high school or at private schools. Another incentive is a discounted rate now offered by many insurance carriers to students who have completed a driver's education program. Some school districts, because of budget cuts, have discontinued their driver's education programs, spurring growth in private instruction.

FOR MORE INFORMATION

For information on driver education, contact the following organizations:

American Driver and Traffic Safety Education Association
Highway Safety Center
Indiana University of Pennsylvania
R&P Building
Indiana, PA 15705
Tel: 800-896-7703
Email: support@hsc.iup.edu
http://www.adtsea.org/adtsea

National Driving Instructors Institute
27762 Forbes Road, Suite 10
Laguna Niguel, CA 92677-1227
Tel: 949-278-5497
Email: info@NDI-Institute
http://www.ndi-institute.com

Inspectors

QUICK FACTS

School Subjects
Mathematics
Technical/shop

Personal Skills
Communication/ideas
Technical/scientific

Work Environment
Indoors and outdoors
Primarily multiple locations

Minimum Education Level
Some postsecondary training

Salary Range
$17,990 to $34,819 to
$52,936+

Certification or Licensing
Voluntary

Outlook
Decline

DOT
168, 620, 736

GOE
08.02.03

NOC
7231, 9482

O*NET-SOC
29-9011.00, 51-9061.00,
53-6051.00

OVERVIEW

Automotive inspectors, sometimes known as *testers*, *quality assurance technicians*, or *quality control inspectors*, inspect automobiles and related components to ensure that they are fit for sale and meet government specifications. Approximately 33,000 inspectors and related works are employed in the U.S. motor vehicle and parts manufacturing industry.

HISTORY

Quality control inspection is an outgrowth of the industrial revolution. As it began in England in the 18th century, each person involved in the manufacturing process was responsible for a particular part of the process. The worker's responsibility was further specialized by the introduction of the concept of interchangeable parts in the late 18th and early 19th centuries. In a manufacturing process using this concept (such as in the automotive industry, for example), a worker could concentrate on making just one component, while other workers concentrated on creating other components. Such specialization led to increased production efficiency, especially as manufacturing processes became mechanized during the early part of the 20th century. It also meant, however, that no one worker was responsible for the overall quality of the product. This led to the need for another kind of specialized production worker whose primary responsibility was not one aspect of the product but rather its overall quality.

This responsibility initially belonged to the mechanical engineers and technicians who developed the manufacturing systems, equipment, and procedures. After World War II, however, a new field emerged that was dedicated solely to quality control. Along with specially trained persons to test and inspect products coming off assembly lines, new instruments, equipment, and techniques were developed to measure and monitor specified standards.

At first, inspectors were primarily responsible for random checks of products to ensure they met all specifications. This usually entailed testing and inspecting either finished products or products at various stages of production.

During the 1980s, a renewed emphasis on quality spread across the United States. Faced with increased global competition, especially from Japanese auto manufacturers, many U.S. automotive companies sought to improve quality and productivity. Quality improvement concepts such as Total Quality Management, Six Sigma, continuous improvement, quality circles, and zero defects gained popularity and changed the way companies viewed quality and quality control practices. A new philosophy emerged, emphasizing quality as the concern of all individuals involved in producing goods and directing that quality be monitored at all stages of manufacturing, not just at the end of production or at random stages of manufacturing.

Today, most automotive companies focus on improving quality during all stages of production, with an emphasis on preventing defects rather than merely identifying defective parts. Inspectors check parts for defects; inspect raw materials such as metals, polymers, fabrics, and chemicals; check the uniformity of subassemblies; and test drive vehicles once they come off the assembly line.

While inspectors still play an important role in the automotive industry, there is an increased use of sophisticated automated equipment that can test and inspect automotive parts and subassemblies as they are manufactured. Automated equipment includes cameras, X rays, lasers, scanners, metal detectors, video inspection systems, electronic sensors, and machine vision systems that can detect the slightest flaw or variance from accepted tolerances. Many companies use statistical process control to record levels of quality and determine the best manufacturing and quality procedures.

THE JOB

Considering each car is made of 15,000 components and about 350 different materials, it's quite a feat to assemble these parts and resources together and end up with a product that is operational, let alone accomplish this with speed, efficiency, and safety. The automotive industry relies on automotive inspectors to ensure that vehicles are properly made and safe to drive according to the standards of the manufacturer, government regulations, and demands of the consumer.

Inspectors often specialize in a certain area or stage of the manufacturing process. For example, an automotive inspector working at Toyota may be in charge of supervising the installation brake systems of a particular vehicle model. They test parts of the system such as the rotors, pads, calipers, or wheel cylinders to be certain each component is made to specification. Inspectors may change a manufacturing or installation process to avoid future defects or deviations in specs. They also run tests on the assembled brake system of a car to determine if it falls within the criteria of Toyota's quality operating system. They often meet with other members of the manufacturing or production team to identify weakness in the design or manufacturing of the vehicle.

Some inspectors test for a vehicle's wear and tear. Inspectors working at Mercedes Benz, for example, may use computerized tests, mechanized tools, or corrosive tests to monitor the strength and durability of different materials used to build a car. They gauge how leather used to construct seating holds up after a series of tests using mechanical tools, checking for tears at the seams, any discoloration, and general aging. They may also use chemicals or other weather simulation tests to check the durability of other parts including car panels, trims, or tires.

Automotive inspectors are often employed by automotive manufacturers, although some may find work with companies that contract out their various inspection services.

Some automotive inspectors are employed by governmental agencies at the local, state, and federal level. *Transportation inspectors* verify not only that vehicles meet safety requirements but also that the personnel who operate the equipment are properly trained to meet the standards regulated by law. *Automobile testers* check the safety and emissions of cars and trucks at state-operated inspection stations. *Occupational safety and health inspectors* enforce the regulations of the Occupational Safety and Health Administration and of state and local governments. Their duties include inspecting machinery, working conditions, and equipment to ensure that proper safety precautions are used that meet government standards and regulations. *Safety health inspectors* make regular visits and also respond to accident reports or complaints about a plant, factory, or other workplace by interviewing workers or management. They may suspend activity that poses a possible threat to workers. They write reports on safety standards that have been violated and describe

An inspector at an automotive manufacturing plant checks measurements on a transaxle. *(Jim West Photography)*

conditions to be corrected. They may also discuss their findings with management to see that standards will be promptly met.

REQUIREMENTS

High School
High school students should focus on general classes in speech; English, especially writing; business; computer science; general mathematics; physics; and shop or vocational training.

Postsecondary Training
Automotive inspectors typically receive on-the-job training, but may also complete two- or four-year degree programs in quality assurance or quality control management. For federal positions, a civil service examination is generally required. Education and experience in the specific field is usually necessary.

Certification or Licensing
Although there are no licensing or certification requirements designed specifically for automotive inspectors, many inspectors pursue the voluntary quality inspector certification from the American Society for Quality. Requirements include having a certain amount of work or educational experience and passing a written examination. Many

employers value this certification and take it into consideration when making new hires or giving promotions.

Other Requirements

Automotive inspectors must be precision-minded, have an eye for detail, and be able to accept responsibility. They also must communicate well with others in order to reach a clear analysis of a situation and be able to report this information to a superior or coworker. Inspectors must be able to write effective reports that convey vast amounts of information and investigative work.

EXPLORING

If you are interested in work as an automotive inspector, you may learn more by talking with people who are employed as inspectors and with your high school counselor. Employment at an automotive plant during summer vacations could be valuable preparation, giving you the opportunity to meet and perhaps talk with inspectors about their careers.

EMPLOYERS

Approximately 28,000 inspectors and related workers are employed in the motor vehicle and parts manufacturing industry in the United States. Other automotive inspectors are employed by local, state, and federal governments.

STARTING OUT

College students may learn of openings for automotive inspectors through their schools' career services office. Recruiters often visit these schools and interview graduating students for technical positions. Students may also learn about openings through help wanted ads or by using the services of state and private employment services. They also may apply directly to automotive manufacturers.

Inspectors who are interested in working for the federal government should visit the Office of Personnel Management's Web site, http://www.usajobs.opm.gov.

ADVANCEMENT

As automotive inspectors gain experience or additional education, they are given more responsible assignments. Promotion usually depends on additional training as well as job performance. Automotive inspectors who obtain additional training have greater chances for advancement opportunities. Inspectors who work for companies with large staffs of inspection personnel can become managers or advance to operations management positions.

Advancement for inspectors in the federal government is based on the civil service promotion and salary structure. Advancement is automatic, usually at one-year intervals, for those people whose work is satisfactory. Additional education may also contribute to advancement to supervisory positions.

EARNINGS

According to the U.S. Department of Labor, inspectors, testers, sorters, samplers, and weighers employed in motor vehicle manufacturing earned median hourly wages of $25.45 in 2006 (or $52,936 annually). Those employed in motor vehicle parts manufacturing earned $16.74 an hour in 2006 (or $34,819 annually). Earnings for all inspectors, testers, sorters, samplers, and weighers ranged from less than $17,990 to $51,690 or more annually in 2006.

Automotive inspectors also receive other benefits including paid vacation and sick days, health and dental insurance, pensions, and life insurance.

WORK ENVIRONMENT

Some automotive inspectors work in manufacturing plants, where conditions may be hot, dirty, and noisy. Others work in laboratories or workshops where they test and inspect raw materials, electronics, and other substances. Because many manufacturing plants operate 24 hours a day, some automotive inspectors may need to work second or third shifts.

OUTLOOK

The U.S. Department of Labor predicts that the employment of inspectors, testers, sorters, samplers, and weighers in motor vehicle and parts manufacturing will decline through 2016 because of increased automation of quality control and testing procedures. Most job opportunities will arise as a result of people retiring, transferring to other positions, and leaving the labor force for a variety of other reasons.

FOR MORE INFORMATION

For information on certification, contact
American Society for Quality
PO Box 3005
Milwaukee, WI 53201-3005
Tel: 800-248-1946
Email: help@asq.org
http://www.asq.org

For information on careers in the federal government, contact
Occupational Safety and Health Administration
http://www.osha.gov

Office of Personnel Management
http://www.usajobs.opm.gov

U.S. Department of Transportation
http://careers.dot.gov

For industry information, contact
National Association of Independent Automotive Inspectors
and Consultants
Email: info@naoiai.com
http://www.naoiai.com

Precision Machinists

OVERVIEW

Precision machinists use machine tools, such as drill presses, lathes, and milling machines, to produce metal parts that meet precise specifications. They combine their knowledge of metals with skillful handling of machine tools to make precision-machined parts for automobiles and other vehicles. Approximately 28,000 precision machinists are employed in the motor vehicle and parts manufacturing industry.

HISTORY

The modern era of producing metal parts accurately and according to specifications began with the invention of the steam engine by James Watt in the latter part of the 18th century. During this same period, John Wilkinson invented the boring machine, which enabled the precise cutting of cylinders for Watt's engine. Also during this time, Henry Maudslay developed a lathe to precisely cut screw threads.

Many other methods of production were developed during the industrial revolution. In Great Britain, metal molds and machine-powered engines were used to produce items that had originally been handcrafted. These new processes lowered costs and sped up production schedules. At about the same time in the United States, Eli Whitney was using tools and machines to make gun parts with such accuracy that they were interchangeable.

This interchangeability of machine-produced parts became the basis for modern mass production. Throughout the 19th century, more specialized and refined metalworking machines were designed.

The electric motor became widely used as a source of power, which spurred further improvements in manufacturing.

The workers who used these machines to create parts—machinists and machine tool operators—developed into a specialized group who combined machining knowledge with skillful handiwork. By 1888, there were enough machinists in various industries to organize their own union.

In the 20th century, the automobile industry was probably the largest single force in the development of machinery and demand for machinists. Technological developments, such as numerical control machinery and computer-aided design applications, have continued to spur progress in machining operations.

These developments have also changed the jobs of machinists. Now workers set manual and computer-controlled machine tools to cut and contour metal into intricate shapes. They use lasers, intricate measuring machines, and modern imaging equipment to check dimensions. Though much of machinists' work is still done by hand, their profession has evolved into much more of a science than a craft.

THE JOB

Precision machinists are trained to operate most types of machine tools that shape pieces of material—usually metal—to specific dimensions. The work done by machine tools can be classified into one of the following categories: cutting, drilling, boring, turning, milling, planing, and grinding.

After receiving a job assignment, the machinist's first task is to review the blueprints or written specifications for the piece to be made (for example, brake rotors, crankshafts, and cylinder blocks). Next the machinist decides which machining operations should be used, plans their sequence, and calculates how fast to feed the metal into the machine. When this is complete, he or she sets up the machine with the proper shaping tools and marks the metal stock (a process called layout work) to indicate where cuts should be made.

Once the layout work is done, the machinist performs the necessary operations. The metal is carefully positioned on the tool, the controls are set, and the cuts are made. During the shaping operation, the machinist constantly monitors the metal feed and the machine speed. If necessary, the machinist adds coolants and lubricants to the workpiece to prevent overheating.

At times machinists produce many identical machined products using a single machine; at other times, they produce one item by working on a variety of machines. After completing machining operations, they may finish the work by hand using files and scrapers, and then assemble finished parts with hand tools.

Machinists' work requires a high degree of accuracy. Some specifications call for accuracy within .0001 of an inch. To achieve this precision, they must use measuring instruments such as scribers, micrometers, calipers, verniers, scales, and gauges.

In the past, machinists had direct control of their machines. However, the increasing use of numerically controlled machines and, in particular, computer numerically controlled machines, has changed the nature of the work. Machinists may now work alone or with tool programmers to program the machines that make the parts. They may also be responsible for checking computer programs to ensure that the machinery is running properly.

Some machinists, often called *production machinists,* may produce large quantities of one part. Others produce relatively small batches of parts or even one-of-a-kind items. Finally, *maintenance machinists* specialize in repairing machinery or making new parts for existing machinery. In repairing a broken part, the maintenance machinist might refer to existing blueprints and perform the same machining operations that were used to create the original part.

REQUIREMENTS

High School

For entry-level jobs most employers prefer high school or vocational school graduates. To prepare yourself for a metalworking career, you should take courses in algebra, geometry, mechanical drawing, blueprint reading, machine shop, drafting, and computer applications. If available, classes in electronics and hydraulics can also be useful.

Postsecondary Training

To become a precision machinist, you need to either complete formal training through an apprenticeship or postsecondary program or receive extensive on-the-job training. Apprenticeships generally consist of four years of shop training combined with related classroom instruction. During shop work, apprentices learn filing, dowel fitting, and the operation of various other machine tools. The operation and programming of computer-controlled tools are also covered. Classroom instruction includes industrial math, blueprint reading, precision machining, computer numerical control concepts, machine tool technology, and manufacturing processes.

You can also enter the field directly from high school or vocational school and receive on-the-job training. In this case newly hired workers are supervised by experienced machinists, training with one machine to another. Trainees usually begin as machine operators. Then, as they show the necessary aptitude, they are given additional training on the machines they are operating. Further instruction in the more technical aspects of machine shop work is obtained through studying manuals and classroom instruction. The amount of progress depends on the skill of the worker.

Certification and Licensing

Increasingly prospective machinists receive postsecondary training through community or technical school programs. Many training facilities have incorporated a set curriculum established by the National Institute for Metalworking Skills (NIMS). After students complete the established courses and pass performance evaluations and written exams, they receive a formal recognition of competency, a NIMS credential. This designation aids in their job search by confirming their skills and knowledge of the metalworking field.

Other Requirements

A precision machinist must have an aptitude for using mechanical principles in practical applications. Knowledge of mathematics and the ability to understand and visualize spatial relationships is also needed to read and interpret engineering drawings.

Machinists must have excellent manual dexterity, good vision and hand-eye coordination, and the concentration and diligence necessary to do highly accurate work. Because their work requires a great deal of standing, lifting, and moving, machinists must also be in good physical condition. Finally, it is necessary for machinists to be able to work independently in an organized, systematic way.

EXPLORING

To observe precision machinists at work, ask a school counselor or teacher to arrange a field trip to a machine shop or an automotive manufacturing plant. You could talk to a machinist personally to learn the pros and cons of their job. Another excellent opportunity to explore this occupation could be through a part-time or summer job in a machine shop or an automotive plant.

EMPLOYERS

Approximately 28,000 precision machinists are employed in the motor vehicle and parts manufacturing industry. They are employed by production engine remanufacturers, machining shops, automotive manufacturers, and auto parts supply houses with machine shop services.

STARTING OUT

To find job leads, try searching newspaper classified sections or contact potential employers directly to ask about opportunities. Other sources of information are state employment offices, the U.S. Department of Labor's Bureau of Apprenticeship and Training, and union headquarters, such as the International Association of Machinists and Aerospace Workers or the International Union, United Automobile, Aerospace, and Agricultural Implement Workers of America. If you receive formal postsecondary training from a community college or technical school, you may find job assistance from the school's career counselors or career services offices.

If you enter the field directly from high school or vocational training, you may be required to start as a machine shop helper or tool operator. These entry-level jobs will help you to develop the experience and technical skills necessary to become a precision machinist.

ADVANCEMENT

After several years of developing their skills, precision machinists have many advancement opportunities. They may choose to specialize in niches such as tool and die design or fabrication, sales, or instrument repairing. In large production shops, machinists have the opportunity to become setup operators or layout workers.

Those who have good judgment, excellent planning skills, and the ability to deal well with people may advance to supervisory positions, such as shop supervisor or plant manager. With additional education, some machinists may become tool engineers. Finally, some skilled and experienced workers eventually go into business for themselves.

EARNINGS

The median hourly salary for precision machinists working in motor vehicle parts manufacturing was $18.27 (or $38,000 annually) in 2006, according to the U.S. Department of Labor. The lowest 10 percent of all precision machinists made less than $10.29 an hour (or $21,400 annually), and the highest 10 percent earned more than $25.31 per hour (or $52,640 annually).

Benefits usually include paid holidays and vacations; life, medical, and accident insurance; and retirement plans.

WORK ENVIRONMENT

Precision machinists generally work 40 hours a week; however, working night and weekend shifts as well as overtime has become more common in the industry as employers increase their hours of production.

Machinists work indoors in shops that are fairly clean, with proper lighting and ventilation. Noise levels are often quite high because of the nature of power-driven machinery. In addition, machining work can be physically strenuous at times. Machinists are usually on their feet for most of the day and are required to lift and maneuver heavy workpieces. For eye protection, they wear safety glasses while using machine tools.

OUTLOOK

Employment for precision machinists employed in motor vehicle and parts manufacturing is expected to decline through 2016, according to the U.S. Department of Labor. Automation is contributing to this slower growth rate. The increased use of computer-controlled machine tools improves efficiency. Therefore, fewer machinists are needed to accomplish the same amount of work.

Even so, openings will arise from the need to replace machinists who retire or transfer to other jobs. In recent years, employers have reported difficulty in attracting skilled workers to machining occupations. If this trend continues, good employment possibilities should exist for candidates with the necessary technical education and skills.

Layoffs are often a factor affecting employment of machinists. When the demand for automobiles and other motor vehicles declines, workers' hours may be either shortened or reduced completely for days, weeks, even months at a time. There is somewhat more job security for maintenance machinists because machines must be cared for even when production is slow.

FOR MORE INFORMATION

For information on apprenticeships, contact
International Association of Machinists and Aerospace Workers
9000 Machinists Place
Upper Marlboro, MD 20772-2687
Tel: 301-967-4500
Email: websteward@goiam.org
http://www.goiam.org

International Union, United Automobile, Aerospace,
  and Agricultural Implement Workers of America
8000 East Jefferson Avenue
Detroit, MI 48214-2699
Tel: 313-926-5000
http://www.uaw.org

For information about skill standards and obtaining NIMS credentials, contact
National Institute for Metalworking Skills (NIMS)
10565 Fairfax Boulevard, Suite 203
Fairfax, VA 22030-3135
Tel: 703-352-4971
http://www.nims-skills.org

For information about training and opportunities in the precision machining and metalworking industries, contact the following organizations:
National Tooling and Machining Association
9300 Livingston Road
Fort Washington, MD 20744-4988
Tel: 800-248-6862
Email: info@ntma.org
http://www.ntma.org

Precision Machined Products Association
6700 West Snowville Road
Brecksville, OH 44141-3292
Tel: 440-526-0300
http://www.pmpa.org

For useful resources about careers and internships in the metalforming industry, contact

Precision Metalforming Association Educational Foundation
6363 Oak Tree Boulevard
Independence, OH 44131-2500
Tel: 216-901-8800
Email: pmaef@pma.org
http://www.metalforming.com/edufound

Visit the Careers in Manufacturing section of the TMA's Web site for more information on careers, wages, and educational recommendations.

Tooling and Manufacturing Association (TMA)
1177 South Dee Road
Park Ridge, IL 60068-4379
Tel: 847-825-1120
http://www.tmanet.org

Precision Metalworkers

OVERVIEW

Precision metalworkers are skilled crafts workers who produce the tools, dies, molds, cutting devices, and guiding and holding devices used in the mass production of a variety of products, including automobiles. *Tool makers* produce precision tools for cutting, shaping, and forming metal and other materials. They also produce jigs and fixtures—the devices for holding the tools and metal while it is being worked—and various gauges and other measuring devices. *Die makers* make precision metal forms, or dies, used in stamping and forging metal. *Mold makers* design and make metal molds for molding plastics, ceramics, and composite materials. In some cases, the term *tool and die maker* is used generically, referring to any or all of these job categories.

HISTORY

The modern machine tool industry came into existence around the beginning of the 19th century. One of the most important early contributors was Eli Whitney, the American inventor and manufacturer who is credited with the first successful use of standardized, interchangeable parts in manufacturing. When Whitney received an order from the U.S. government in 1798 for thousands of muskets, he envisioned a new work method. He realized that he could design machines that would allow unskilled workers to turn out many identical copies of each part in a musket. In carrying out his plan, he invented jigs (tool-guiding patterns) and fixtures (devices that clamp workpieces in place). They were the first versions of devices that are very important in today's tool and die making.

Another significant invention of the 19th century was the power press, which could be fitted with presswork dies, or stamping dies, to cut and form items out of sheet metal. Today, the fabrication of presswork dies remains an important part of tool and die making. Other significant developments in the field have included methods for die-casting metals and injection-molding materials, such as plastics.

The rapid growth of mass production techniques in the late 19th century spurred the development of tool and die shops, mostly small, independent contractors, who today employ the majority of precision metalworkers in the United States. Also, as manufacturing industries (including the automotive industry) came to use more kinds of precision tools and dies, the workers who fabricate them have become increasingly specialized. So, even though today's tools and dies make hundreds of thousands of mass-produced parts, they themselves must be custom made by highly skilled crafts workers. Today's tooling shops typically perform a few very sophisticated types of tasks, rather than a broad range of tool making and die making.

THE JOB

Tool, die, and mold makers are among the most highly skilled production workers in the economy. They possess a broad knowledge of machining operations, can read complex blueprints, and are able to do complicated mathematical calculations. They may put together several parts to form subassemblies, and then put the subassemblies together to build an entire vehicle. In a small shop, a single worker is typically responsible for all the steps necessary to complete a part from start to finish, while in a larger shop, specialized production tasks are allocated among several workers, with the tool maker or die maker acting as a job supervisor.

Many types of machine shops and workers are covered under the tool and die category. They include tool and die shops that produce dies, punches, die sets and components, subpresses, jigs and fixtures, and special checking devices. Also included are companies that manufacture molds for die-casting and foundry casting, and shops that make metal molds for plastics, rubber, plaster, and glass working.

In general, pressworking dies are used to cut and shape sheet metals with electrical or hydraulic presses. Composed of two units, the upper part attaches to a press ram and the lower part attaches to a press bed. Molding dies, used to form both metals and plastics, consist of two units which when closed form a cavity into which molten material is poured.

No matter what the shop produces, however, when a job first arrives, the tool and die makers must analyze instructions, blueprints, sketches, or models of the finished product. Using such information, they decide how to go about making the device. After the dimensions are computed, tool and die makers plan the layout and assembly processes and decide on a sequence of operations for machining the metal.

When the plan is clear, workers select and lay out metal stock, measuring and marking the metal, and if necessary, cutting it into pieces of the approximate size needed for the project. They set up the machine tools, such as lathes, drill presses, and grinders, and carefully cut, bore, and drill the metal according to their predetermined plan. In the machining process, they closely monitor the dimensions of the workpiece since their work must have a high degree of accuracy—frequently within ten-thousandths of an inch. Measuring equipment, such as micrometers, gauge blocks, and dial indicators, is used to ensure precision.

When satisfied that the parts are accurately machined in accordance with the original specifications, tool and die makers fit the pieces together to make the final product. They may need to do finishing work on the product, such as filing and smoothing surfaces. Depending on the size and complexity of the device, the production process may take weeks or months to complete.

Modern technology is changing the way tools are developed and produced. Firms now commonly use computer-aided design to develop products and parts, and to design the tooling to make the parts. These tool drawings are then processed by a computer program to calculate cutting paths and the sequence of operations. Once these instructions are developed, computer numerical control tool machines are usually used to produce the individual components of the tool. Often, these programs are stored for future use.

REQUIREMENTS

High School
Applicants for jobs in this field need to have at least a high school or vocational school education. Courses in mathematics, blueprint reading, drafting, computers, metalworking, and machine shop are very useful.

Postsecondary Training

Precision metalworkers can learn their trade either through informal on-the-job training or formal apprenticeships, which most employers prefer because of the thoroughness of the training. Lasting four to five years, apprenticeships combine a planned and supervised on-the-job training program with class work in related fields. On the job, apprentices learn how to set up and operate machine tools, such as lathes, milling machines, grinders, and jig borers. They also learn to use other mechanical equipment, gauges, and various hand tools. In addition, they receive classroom instruction in blueprint reading, mechanical drawing, tool programming, shop theory, shop mathematics, properties of various metals, and tool design.

Workers who become on-the-job trainees are initially assigned simple tasks that usually involve operating machines; later they are given increasingly more complex work. They pick up skills gradually. One drawback to this method is that it may take many years to learn all the necessary skills.

Tool and die makers or mold makers may start out as machinists. They supplement their metalworking experience with additional training, which may include layout work, shop mathematics, blueprint reading, heat-treating, and the use of precision tools, through vocational or correspondence schools.

Certification and Licensing

Many apprenticeship-training facilities have incorporated a set curriculum established by the National Institute for Metalworking Skills (NIMS). After students complete the established courses and pass performance evaluations and written exams, they receive a formal recognition of competency, a NIMS credential. This designation aids in their job search by confirming their skills and knowledge of the metalworking field.

Other Requirements

Precision metalworkers have a mechanical aptitude and the ability to work with careful attention to detail. To ensure the absolute precision of their work, they are very methodical and continuously check measurements of the workpiece throughout the job. Workers also need to be able to work as efficiently as possible, with a minimum waste of time or materials. Good eyesight is a must, and in some jobs, workers must be able to lift moderately heavy objects.

Because they often work without close supervision, tool and die makers need to be self-motivated and organized in their work habits. In addition, they need good communication skills to help them work in cooperation with others.

EXPLORING

There are several ways to learn about precision metalworking. Hobbies such as tinkering with cars, making models, and assembling electronic equipment may be helpful in testing patience, accuracy, and mechanical ability, all of which are important qualities for tool and die makers. A field trip to a mold shop, tool and die shop, or automotive manufacturing plant can give you a glimpse of the work in this field and may offer the opportunity to talk to experienced workers. Even better is a part-time or summer job in such a setting. Although your work would probably be basic labor, such as sweeping floors, the experience could provide a valuable opportunity to observe firsthand the day-to-day activities in a machine shop.

EMPLOYERS

Most precision metalworkers are employed in independent job shops where tools and dies are tailor-made for a variety of manufacturers. These shops are generally located in the Midwest, Northeast, and West. The largest concentration is in Michigan. Precision metalworkers also work in industries that manufacture machines and equipment for metalworking, automobiles, and other motor vehicles, aircraft, and plastics products. Among large manufacturers, such as automakers, however, there seems to be a trend to close in-house shops.

STARTING OUT

Information about apprentice programs and job openings for prospective precision metalworkers is available from various sources. These include the state employment offices; local employers, such as tool and die shops and manufacturing firms; various metalworking trade associations; and the local offices of unions, such as the United Auto Workers or the International Association of Machinists and Aerospace Workers. Additionally, high school, vocational school, and technical institute students may get help from their teachers or the career services office at their schools.

ADVANCEMENT

After completing apprenticeship training, workers often need several more years of experience to learn the most difficult and specialized skills. Well-qualified, experienced workers may have several avenues of advancement open to them. With today's shortage of precision metalworkers, opportunities are plentiful for those who have good experience. Some may choose to move into a larger shop for more pay or accept a supervisory position. Others may decide to become a tool designer or specialist in programming computer numerical control tool machines.

Another possibility for some tool makers is to become a tool inspector in an industry that requires a particularly high degree of accuracy in components. Many workers go into business for themselves, opening their own independent job shops to make items for manufacturing firms that do not maintain their own tool-making or die-making department.

EARNINGS

Earnings for tool and die makers are generally good. According to the U.S. Department of Labor, the mean annual wage for those employed in motor vehicle parts manufacturing was $53,630 in 2006. The lowest 10 percent of all tool and die makers earned less than $28,810, while the top 10 percent earned more than $67,420. Workers in mold making in the motor vehicle parts manufacturing industry earned a mean salary of $31,940 in 2006. Salaries for mold makers in all industries ranged from less than $16,890 to $40,270 or more.

In addition to regular earnings, most precision metalworkers receive benefits such as health insurance, paid vacation days, and retirement plans.

WORK ENVIRONMENT

Precision metalworkers typically work 40 hours per week, although overtime is not unusual. Most plants that employ these workers operate only one shift per day. They usually work in shops that are adequately lighted, temperature-controlled, and well ventilated. Their work areas are not typically very noisy, as opposed to production departments. There are exceptions, however—tool and die departments that are near production areas or heat-treating or casting areas may be hot and noisy. Workers spend much of the day standing and moving about, and they may occasionally have to lift moderately heavy objects.

To avoid injury from machines and flying bits of metal, workers must follow good safety practices and use appropriate protective gear, including safety glasses and hearing protectors. In some settings, workers are exposed to smoky conditions, and they may get oil, coolants, and other irritating substances on their skin.

Since most precision metalworkers work on a variety of projects, their work is seldom routine. In some cases, workers are completing several jobs at once. Many who choose this field find the work to be very satisfying. They typically work with little supervision. They also have the pleasure of seeing a project through from start to finish and knowing that they have done a precise and skillful job.

OUTLOOK

Although employers report difficulty in finding skilled workers for their jobs, the employment of precision metalworkers is expected to decline through 2016, according to the U.S. Department of Labor. More numerically controlled machine tools and other automated equipment are being used so fewer operations are being done by hand, resulting in fewer workers being needed. Furthermore, some products that are mass produced using tools and dies are being imported from abroad, as are some tools and dies. China, for example, is becoming a competitor in the tool and die-making field, although their technology is not yet at the level of shops here.

Despite this employment prediction, openings are still available for new workers each year. Many of the workers presently employed in these occupations are approaching retirement, which will result in job openings. Many more openings will occur due to individuals advancing into other fields. Employers in almost every area of the country are experiencing significant trouble filling positions, according to several trade associations. Highly skilled workers can continue to expect to have very good job opportunities if the shortage grows more acute.

These crafts workers play a key role in the operation of many firms. As firms continue to invest in new equipment and modify production techniques, they will continue to rely heavily on skilled tool and die makers for retooling. This, coupled with the growing demand for products that use machined parts, should help to keep demand constant for qualified precision metalworkers.

FOR MORE INFORMATION

For information on training and apprenticeships in precision metalworking, contact the following:

International Union of Electronic, Electrical, Salaried, Machine, and Furniture Workers-Communications Workers of America
501 Third Street, NW
Washington, DC 20001-2797
Tel: 202-434-1100
http://www.iue-cwa.org

International Union, United Automobile, Aerospace, and Agricultural Implement Workers of America
8000 East Jefferson Avenue
Detroit, MI 48214-2699
Tel: 313-926-5000
http://www.uaw.org

For industry information, contact
American Mold Builders Association
701 East Irving Park Road, Suite 207
Roselle, IL 60172-2357
Tel: 630-980-7667
Email: info@amba.org
http://www.amba.org

For information about skill standards and obtaining NIMS credentials, contact
National Institute for Metalworking Skills (NIMS)
10565 Fairfax Boulevard, Suite 203
Fairfax, VA 22030-3135
Tel: 703-352-4971
Email: nims@nims-skills.org
http://www.nims-skills.org

For information about training and opportunities in the precision machining and metalworking industries, contact
National Tooling and Machining Association
9300 Livingston Road
Fort Washington, MD 20744-4988
Tel: 800-248-6862
Email: info@ntma.org
http://www.ntma.org

For useful resources about careers and internships in the metalforming industry, contact
Precision Metalforming Association Educational Foundation
6363 Oak Tree Boulevard
Independence, OH 44131-2500
Tel: 216-901-8800
Email: pmaef@pma.org
http://www.metalforming.com/edufound

Visit the Careers in Manufacturing section of the TMA's Web site for more information on careers, wages, and educational recommendations.

Tooling and Manufacturing Association (TMA)
1177 South Dee Road
Park Ridge, IL 60068-4379
Tel: 847-825-1120
http://www.tmanet.org

Public Relations Specialists

QUICK FACTS

School Subjects
Business
English
Journalism

Personal Skills
Communication/ideas
Leadership/management
Technical/scientific

Work Environment
Primarily indoors
One location with some
   travel

Minimum Education Level
Bachelor's degree

Salary Range
$28,080 to $47,350 to
$89,220+

Certification or Licensing
Voluntary

Outlook
About as fast as the average

DOT
165

GOE
01.03.01

NOC
5124

O*NET-SOC
11-2031.00, 27-3031.00

OVERVIEW

Public relations (PR) specialists employed in the automotive industry develop and maintain programs that present a favorable public image for an automotive manufacturer, automobile dealer, or professional automotive association.

PR specialists may be employed by corporations, government agencies, nonprofit organizations, or almost any type of organization. Many PR specialists hold positions in public relations consulting firms or work for advertising agencies. Of the approximately 243,000 public relations specialists in the United States, a small percentage are employed in the automotive industry.

HISTORY

The first public relations counsel was a reporter named Ivy Ledbetter Lee, who in 1906 was named press representative for a group of coalmine operators. Labor disputes were becoming a large concern of the operators, and they had run into problems because of their continual refusal to talk to the press and the hired miners. Lee convinced the mine operators to start responding to press questions and supply the press with information on the mine activities.

During and after World War II, the rapid advancement of communications techniques prompted firms to realize they needed professional help to ensure their messages were given proper public attention. Manufacturing firms that had converted their production facilities to the war effort returned to the manufacture of peacetime products and enlisted the aid of public relations professionals to forcefully and convincingly bring products and the company name before the buying public.

Large business firms, labor unions, and service organizations, such as the American Red Cross, Boy Scouts of America, and the YMCA, began to recognize the value of establishing positive, healthy relationships with the public that they served and depended on for support. The need for effective public relations was often emphasized when circumstances beyond a company's or institution's control created unfavorable reactions from the public.

Public relations specialists must be experts at representing their clients before the media. The rapid growth of the public relations field since 1945 is testimony to the increased awareness in all industries of the need for professional attention to the proper use of media and the proper public relations approach to the many publics of a firm or an organization—customers, employees, stockholders, contributors, and competitors.

Public relations specialists play an important role in the automotive industry by presenting it in the best manner to potential customers, stockholders, lawmakers, and others in the industry. Some examples of good public relations might include touting an automotive company's community outreach programs or efforts to create environmentally friendly vehicles and manufacturing processes. Public relations specialists also conduct damage control in the wake of bad news such as financial problems, performance issues with vehicles, and other potentially negative situations.

In 1974, the Automotive Public Relations Council was founded to represent the professional interests of public relations specialists in the automotive industry.

THE JOB

Public relations specialists are employed to do a variety of tasks. They may be employed primarily as writers, creating reports, news releases, and booklet texts. Others write speeches or create copy for radio, TV, or film sequences. These workers often spend much of their time contacting the press, radio, and TV as well as magazines on behalf of the employer. Some PR specialists work more as editors than writers, fact-checking and rewriting employee publications, newsletters, shareholder reports, and other management communications.

Specialists may choose to concentrate in graphic design, using their background knowledge of art and layout for developing brochures, booklets, and photographic communications. Other PR workers handle special events, such as press parties, convention exhibits, open houses, or anniversary celebrations.

PR specialists must be alert to any and all company or institutional events that are newsworthy. They prepare news releases and direct them toward the proper media. Specialists working for manufacturers and retailers are concerned with efforts that will promote sales and create goodwill for the firm's products. They work closely with the marketing and sales departments in announcing new products (such as a new car model or feature), preparing displays, and attending occasional dealers' conventions and automobile shows.

A large firm may have a director of public relations who is a vice president of the company and in charge of a staff that includes writers, artists, researchers, and other specialists. Publicity for an individual or a small company may involve many of the same areas of expertise but may be carried out by a few people or possibly even one person.

Many PR workers act as consultants (rather than staff) of an automotive manufacturer or dealer, association, college, hospital, or other institution. These workers have the advantage of being able to operate independently, state opinions objectively, and work with more than one type of business or association.

PR specialists are called upon to work with the public opinion aspects of almost every corporate or institutional problem. These can range from the opening of a new manufacturing plant, to the introduction of a new eco-friendly automotive hybrid, to a merger or sale of a company.

Public relations professionals may specialize. *Lobbyists* try to persuade legislators and other office holders to pass laws favoring the interests of the firms or people they represent (such as arguing against the implementation of fuel efficiency standards or lobbying legislators for approval of a new automotive plant despite opposition by certain public interest groups).

Early in their careers, public relations specialists become accustomed to having others receive credit for their behind-the-scenes work. The speeches they draft will be delivered by company officers, the magazine articles they prepare may be credited to the president of the company, and they may be consulted to prepare the message to stockholders from the chairman of the board that appears in the annual report.

REQUIREMENTS

High School

While in high school, take courses in English, journalism, public speaking, humanities, and languages because public relations is based on effective communication with others. Courses such as these will develop your skills in written and oral communication as well as provide a better understanding of different fields and industries to be publicized.

Postsecondary Training

Most people employed in public relations service have a college degree. Major fields of study most beneficial to developing the proper skills are public relations, English, and journalism. Some employers feel that majoring in the area in which the public relations person will eventually work is the best training. For example, those interested in working in the automotive industry might consider taking classes or even pursuing a degree in automotive engineering, design, technology, or a related field. A knowledge of business administration is most helpful as is a native talent for selling. A graduate degree may be required for managerial positions. People with a bachelor's degree in public relations can find staff positions with either an organization or a public relations firm.

More than 200 colleges and about 100 graduate schools offer degree programs or special courses in public relations. In addition, many other colleges offer at least courses in the field. Public relations programs are sometimes administered by the journalism or communication departments of schools. In addition to courses in theory and techniques of public relations, interested individuals may study organization, management and administration, and practical applications and often specialize in areas such as business, government, and nonprofit organizations. Other preparation includes courses in creative writing, psychology, communications, advertising, and journalism.

Certification or Licensing

The Public Relations Society of America and the International Association of Business Communicators accredit public relations workers who have at least five years of experience in the field and pass a comprehensive examination. Such accreditation is a sign of competence in this field, although it is not a requirement for employment.

Other Requirements

Today's public relations specialist must be a businessperson first, both to understand how to perform successfully in business and to comprehend the needs and goals of the organization or client. Additionally, the public relations specialist needs to be a strong writer and speaker, with good interpersonal, leadership, and organizational skills.

EXPLORING

Almost any experience in working with other people will help you to develop strong interpersonal skills, which are crucial in public relations. The possibilities are almost endless. Summer work on a newspaper or trade paper or with a radio or television station may give insight into communications media. Working as a volunteer on a political campaign can help you to understand the ways in which people can be persuaded. Being selected as a page for the U.S. Congress or a state legislature will help you grasp the fundamentals of government processes. A job in retail will help you to understand some of the principles of product presentation. A teaching job will develop your organization and presentation skills. These are just some of the jobs that will let you explore areas of public relations.

If you are interested in working in the automotive industry, try to land a part-time job in the public relations department of an automotive manufacturer. You should also visit the Web sites of major automotive manufacturers such as Ford, General Motors, and Chrysler to read press releases and other material prepared by public relations specialists. You could even contact a public relations specialist at one of these Web sites to see if he or she would be interested in participating in an information interview.

EMPLOYERS

Public relations specialists hold about 243,000 jobs, but only a small percentage of this number are employed in the automotive industry. Workers may be paid employees of the organization they represent or they may be part of a public relations firm that works for organizations on a contract basis. Some major employers of PR specialists in the automotive industry include General Motors, Ford Motor Company, Chrysler LLC, Honda, Nissan, Toyota, Hyundai, Volkswagen, BMW, and Mercedes-Benz. Other PR specialists work for large automobile dealers or for industry organizations such as the National Automobile Dealers Association or the Automotive Aftermarket Industry Association.

STARTING OUT

No clear-cut formula exists for getting a job in public relations. Individuals often enter the field after gaining preliminary experience in another occupation closely allied to the field, usually some segment of communications, and frequently, in journalism. Coming into public relations from newspaper work is still a recommended route. Another good method is to gain initial employment as a public relations trainee or intern, or as a clerk, secretary, or research assistant in a public relations department or a counseling firm.

If you are interested in working in the automotive industry, visit the Web sites of large companies such as Ford to learn more job openings. You can also learn more about jobs through the career services office at your college.

ADVANCEMENT

In some large companies, an entry-level public relations specialist may start as a trainee in a formal training program for new employees. In others, new employees may expect to be assigned to work that has a minimum of responsibility. They may assemble clippings or do rewrites on material that has already been accepted. They may make posters or assist in conducting polls or surveys, or compile reports from data submitted by others.

As workers acquire experience, they are typically given more responsibility. They write news releases, direct polls or surveys, or advance to writing speeches for company officials. Progress may seem to be slow, because some skills take a long time to master.

Some advance in responsibility and salary in the same firm in which they started. Others find that the path to advancement is to accept a more rewarding position in another firm or at a larger automotive company.

The goal of many public relations specialists is to open an independent office or to join an established consulting firm. To start an independent office requires a large outlay of capital and an established reputation in the field. However, those who are successful in operating their own consulting firms probably attain the greatest financial success in the public relations field.

EARNINGS

Public relations specialists employed in all fields had median annual earnings of $47,350 in 2006, according to the U.S. Department of Labor. Salaries ranged from less than $28,080 to more than $89,220.

Many PR workers receive a range of fringe benefits from corporations and agencies employing them, including bonus/incentive compensation, stock options, profit sharing/pension plans/401(k) programs, medical benefits, life insurance, financial planning, maternity/paternity leave, paid vacations, and family college tuition. Bonuses can range from 5 to 100 percent of base compensation and often are based on individual and/or company performance.

WORK ENVIRONMENT

Public relations specialists generally work in offices with adequate secretarial help, regular salary increases, and expense accounts. They are expected to make a good appearance in tasteful, conservative clothing. They must have social poise, and their conduct in their personal life is important to their firms or their clients. The public relations specialist may have to entertain business associates.

The PR specialist seldom works conventional office hours for many weeks at a time; although the workweek may consist of 35 to 40 hours, these hours may be supplemented by evenings and even weekends when meetings must be attended and other special events covered. Time behind the desk may represent only a small part of the total working schedule. Travel is often an important and necessary part of the job.

The life of the PR worker is so greatly determined by the job that many consider this a disadvantage. Because the work is concerned with public opinion, it is often difficult to measure the results of performance and to sell the worth of a public relations program to an employer or client. Competition in the consulting field is keen, and if a firm loses an account, some of its personnel may be affected. The demands it makes for anonymity will be considered by some as one of the profession's less inviting aspects. Public relations involves much more hard work and a great deal less glamour than is popularly supposed.

OUTLOOK

Overall employment in the motor vehicle and parts manufacturing industry is predicted to decline by 14 percent through 2016, according to the U.S. Department of Labor. Despite this prediction, employment opportunities should continue to be available at automotive companies and dealerships. With competition extremely strong in this industry, it is extremely important for companies to have effective public relations workers so that the public continues to have a positive opinion of the company—and continues to purchase vehicles. All automotive companies have some sort of public relations resource, either through their own staff or through the use of a firm of consultants. Most are expected to expand their public relations activities, creating many new jobs.

Employment of public relations professionals in all fields is expected to grow faster than average for all other occupations through 2016, according to the U.S. Department of Labor. Competition will be keen for beginning jobs in public relations because so many job seekers are enticed by the perceived glamour and appeal of the field; those with both education and experience will have an advantage.

FOR MORE INFORMATION

For industry information, contact
Automotive Public Relations Council
10 Laboratory Drive
Research Triangle Park, NC 27709
Tel: 919-406-8828
http://www.aprc-online.org

For information on accreditation, contact
International Association of Business Communicators
One Hallidie Plaza, Suite 600
San Francisco, CA 94102-2842
Tel: 415-544-4700
http://www.iabc.com

For statistics, salary surveys, and information on accreditation and student membership, contact
Public Relations Society of America
33 Maiden Lane, 11th Floor
New York, NY 10038-5150
Tel: 212-460-1400
Email: prssa@prsa.org (student membership)
http://www.prsa.org

Teachers, Automotive Training

QUICK FACTS

School Subjects
Speech
Technical/shop

Personal Skills
Mechanical/manipulative
Helping/teaching

Work Environment
Primarily indoors
Primarily one location

Minimum Education Level
Associate's degree

Salary Range
$25,420 to $46,000 to
$73,610+

Certification or Licensing
Required (secondary
teachers)
None available (college
teachers)

Outlook
Decline (secondary teachers)
Much faster than the average
(college teachers)

DOT
097

GOE
12.03.02, 12.03.03

NOC
4131, 4141

O*NET-SOC
25-1194.00, 25-2032.00

OVERVIEW

Automotive teachers instruct students regarding automotive-related subjects at high schools and colleges and universities. They lecture classes, conduct hands-on instruction in repair shops and laboratories, and create and grade examinations. They also may conduct research, write for publication, and aid in administration.

HISTORY

In American colonial times, organized adult education was started to help people make up for schooling missed as children or to help people prepare for jobs. Apprenticeships were an early form of vocational education in the American colonies as individuals were taught a craft by working with a skilled person in a particular field. Training programs continued to develop as carpenters, bricklayers, and other craftspeople learned their skills through vocational training courses.

In 1911, Wisconsin established the first State Board of Vocational and Adult Education in the country, and in 1917 the federal government supported the continuing education movement by funding vocational training in public schools for individuals over the age of 14. Immediately after World War II, the federal government took another large stride in financial support of adult and vocational education by creating the

G.I. Bill of Rights, which provided money for veterans to pursue further job training.

Today colleges and universities, vocational high schools, private trade schools, private businesses, and other organizations offer adults the opportunity to prepare for a specific occupation, such as automotive technology or collision repair, or pursue personal enrichment.

The National Association of College Automotive Teachers (now known as the North American Council of Automotive Teachers) was founded in 1977 to serve the professional needs of automotive teachers.

THE JOB

In the classroom, high school automotive teachers instruct students regarding a variety of automotive-related subjects such as brakes, electrical systems, collision repair, suspension and steering, heating and air-conditioning systems, and engine repair. They spend a great deal of time lecturing, but also teach students via hands-on training in on-site repair facilities. Outside of the classroom and repair shop, high school automotive teachers prepare lectures, lesson plans, and exams. They evaluate student work and calculate grades. In the process of planning their class, secondary school teachers read textbooks and workbooks to determine reading assignments; photocopy notes, articles, and other handouts; and develop grading policies. They also continue to study alternative and traditional teaching methods to hone their skills. They prepare students for special events and conferences and submit student work to competitions.

College automotive instructors teach at junior and technical colleges or at four-year colleges and universities. They cover a wide variety of subjects ranging from automotive repair technology, to automotive engineering, to automotive design. Typical classes taught by college automotive teachers include Introduction to Collision Repair, Introduction to Automotive Engine Repair, Welding for Automotive Mechanics, Basic Automotive Air Conditioning, Introduction to Automotive Engineering, Adapters/Tools/Measurements, Interior Body Construction, Auto Collision Welding, Frame and Unibody Damage Analysis, Steering/Suspension, Color-Matching, Basic Automotive Electricity, Automotive Maintenance and Inspection Procedures, Automotive Engine Performance Diagnosis, Automotive Brake Systems, Automotive Drive Lines and Repair Procedures, Hybrid Engines, and Introduction to Alternative Fuel Cell Technology.

College automotive instructors' most important responsibility is to teach students. Their role within a college department will determine the level of courses they teach and the number of courses per semester. They may head several classes a semester or only a few a year. Some of their classes will have large enrollment, while advanced seminars may consist of only 12 or fewer students.

Though college automotive teachers may spend fewer than 10 to 15 hours a week in the actual classroom, they spend many hours preparing lectures and lesson plans, grading papers and exams, preparing grade reports, and readying the repair shops for classes. They also schedule office hours during the week to be available to students outside of class, and they meet with students individually throughout the semester. In the classroom, teachers lecture, lead discussions, administer exams, and assign textbook reading and other research. They also teach students in an industrial setting, or repair shop, that allows students to get hands-on experience repairing automobile engines, fixing collision damage, or using welding tools to fabricate auto parts.

In addition to teaching, most college automotive teachers conduct research and write publications. Professors publish their research findings in various industry journals. They also write books based on their research or on their own knowledge and experience in the field.

REQUIREMENTS

High School
Your high school's college preparatory program likely includes courses in English, science, foreign language, history, math, and government. In addition, you should take courses in speech to get a sense of what it will be like to lecture to a group of students. Your school's debate team can also help you develop public speaking skills, along with research skills. You should take as many automotive technology classes as possible.

Postsecondary Training
If you want to teach at the high school level, you may choose to major in your subject area while taking required education courses, or you may major in secondary education with a concentration in automotive technology. You will also need to student teach in an actual classroom environment.

For prospective professors, you will need at least one degree in your chosen field of study—automotive technology, engineering,

A student in a college automotive technology program uses computer technology to help diagnose a problem with a vehicle. *(James Marshall, The Image Works)*

design, or a related field. If you plan on teaching a hard science, such as automotive engineering, you will need at least a master's degree to work as a professor.

Other Requirements

To be a successful automotive teacher, you need to be an expert in automotive technology and related fields. People skills are important because you'll be dealing directly with students, administrators, and other faculty members on a daily basis. You should feel comfortable in a role of authority and possess self-confidence.

EXPLORING

Start learning about this career by talking to your high school automotive technology teachers about their careers. Work on cars to gain valuable firsthand experience. An after-school job in a repair shop or dealership can give you an introduction to the world of automotives. You can develop your own teaching experience by volunteering at a community center, or working at a summer camp, or teaching a friend how to do a basic car repair. Also, spend some time on a college campus to get a sense of the environment. Write to colleges for their admissions brochures and course catalogs (or check them out online); read about the faculty members and the courses they teach. Before visiting college campuses, make arrangements to speak to automotive instructors who teach courses that interest you. These educators may allow you to sit in on their classes and observe.

EMPLOYERS

Automotive teachers are employed at high schools, vocational and technical colleges, and colleges and universities. Although rural areas maintain schools, more teaching positions are available in urban or suburban areas.

STARTING OUT

Secondary school automotive teachers can use their college career services offices and state departments of education to find job openings. Many local schools advertise teaching positions in newspapers. Another option is to directly contact the administration in the schools in which you'd like to work. While looking for a full-time position, you can work as a substitute teacher. In more urban areas with many schools, you may be able to find full-time substitute work.

Many students begin applying for postsecondary teaching positions while finishing their college program. Some professional associations maintain lists of teaching opportunities in their areas. They may also make lists of applicants available to college administrators looking to fill an available position.

ADVANCEMENT

As secondary teachers acquire experience or additional education, they can expect higher wages and more responsibilities. Teachers with leadership skills and an interest in administrative work may advance to serve as principals or supervisors, though the number of these positions is limited and competition is fierce. Another move may be into higher education, teaching education classes at a college or university. For most of these positions, additional education is required.

At the postsecondary level, the normal pattern of advancement is from instructor to assistant professor, to associate professor, to full professor. College faculty members who have an interest in and a talent for administration may be advanced to chair of a department or to dean of their college. Many automotive instructors continue to work in their chosen field—for example, as an automotive mechanic, engineer, or collision repair specialists—while working as teachers.

EARNINGS

The median annual salary for secondary vocational education teachers was $48,690 in 2006, according to the U.S. Department of Labor. The lowest 10 percent earned less than $33,070; the highest 10 percent earned $73,280 or more. The median salary for postsecondary vocational education teachers was $43,900 in 2006, with 10 percent earning $73,610 or more, and 10 percent earning $25,420 or less.

Benefits for full-time teachers typically include health insurance and retirement funds and, in some cases, stipends for travel related to research, housing allowances, and tuition waivers for dependents.

WORK ENVIRONMENT

Most teachers are contracted to work 10 months out of the year, with a two-month vacation during the summer. During their summer break, many continue their education to renew or upgrade their teaching licenses (for secondary school teachers) and earn higher salaries. Teachers in schools that operate year-round work eight-week sessions with one-week breaks in between and a five-week vacation in the winter.

Teachers work in generally pleasant conditions, although some older schools may have poor heating or electrical systems. The work can seem confining, requiring them to remain in the classroom throughout most of the day.

High school hours are generally held from 8 a.m. to 3 p.m., but teachers work more than 40 hours a week teaching, preparing for classes, grading papers, and directing extracurricular activities. Similarly, most college teachers work more than 40 hours each week. Although they may teach only two or three classes a semester, they spend many hours preparing for lectures, examining student work, and conducting research.

Depending on the size of the department, college teachers may have their own office, or they may have to share an office with one or more colleagues. Their department may provide them with a computer, Internet access, and research assistants. College teachers can arrange their schedule around class hours, academic meetings, and the established office hours when they meet with students.

OUTLOOK

According to the *Occupational Outlook Handbook*, employment opportunities for vocational education teachers at the secondary level are expected to decline through 2016. Despite this prediction, the need to replace retiring teachers will provide opportunities nationwide.

The U.S. Department of Labor predicts excellent employment growth for college vocational education teachers through 2016 due to a growing emphasis on career and technical education at this level. College enrollment is projected to grow due to an increased number of 18- to 24-year-olds, adults returning to college, and foreign-born students. Retirement of current faculty members will also provide job openings.

FOR MORE INFORMATION

To read about the issues affecting college professors, contact
American Association of University Professors
1012 14th Street, NW, Suite 500
Washington, DC 20005-3406
Tel: 202-737-5900
Email: aaup@aaup.org
http://www.aaup.org

For information about careers and current issues affecting teachers, contact or visit the Web sites of the following organizations:
American Federation of Teachers
555 New Jersey Avenue, NW
Washington, DC 20001-2029
Tel: 202-879-4400
http://www.aft.org

National Education Association
1201 16th Street, NW
Washington, DC 20036-3290
Tel: 202-833-4000
http://www.nea.org

For industry information, contact
Association for Career and Technical Education
1410 King Street
Alexandria, VA 22314-2749

Tel: 800-826-9972
http://www.acteonline.org and http://www.acteonline.org/
   career/skills

For information on a career as an automotive teacher, contact
North American Council of Automotive Teachers
11956 Bernardo Plaza Drive, PMB 436
San Diego, CA 92128-2538
Tel: 858-487-8126
Email: nacat@cts.com
http://www.nacat.com

INTERVIEW

Mike Dommer is an instructor of automotive technology at Indian Hills Community College (IHCC, http://www.ihcc.cc.ia.us) in Iowa. He discussed the field with the editors of Careers in Focus: Automotives.

Q. **Tell us about your program and your background.**

A. Our program is 18-months in length. Upon successful completion the student receives an A.A.S. degree in automotive technology. Students who do not complete the whole program to include the transferable arts and science courses receive certificates for the technical courses they have completed. Our program is year-round; we do not break in the summer. One of the unique things about our school is that we have a four-day school week. This is a pretty good incentive for our students who have part-time jobs.

   I completed the "auto mechanics" one-year diploma program here at IHCC in 1972. During high school I worked at a local full-service gas station that did all types of mechanical repairs on cars and trucks. From 1972 until 1993 I worked as an automotive technician and later as a service manager in General Motors/Chrysler dealerships. I owned and operated my own shop from 1988 to 1990. I am ASE certified as a master automotive tech. I also hold ASE certifications in L1 automotive advanced performance, parts, service advisor, and undercar specialist.

   I have been in the Iowa Army National Guard for 30 years. My experiences there are as a combat engineer officer and as a maintenance technician. I have been mobilized/deployed twice in my career. The most recent was from February 2003–June 2004. During that time I was the maintenance supervisor for a transportation company with more than 70 tactical cargo trucks and tractors, many of which were built in the 1970s. I was also responsible for the maintenance and repair of all the other unit equipment to include generators and individual and crew-served weapons.

Q. What is one thing that young people may not know about a career in automotive technology?

A. Many of our students are unaware of the technical knowledge that is required of today's automotive technicians. It seems like some are guided into the career field by counselors or relatives who do not have a very good understanding about how the career field has transformed over the past 20 to 30 years.

Q. What made you want to become an automotive technology teacher?

A. As a service manager working in dealerships I was frustrated with the difficulty in hiring qualified auto techs, even at the entry level. Idealistically, I thought I might be able to impact that shortage by being involved in the education process.

Q. What advice would you offer automotive technology majors as they graduate and look for jobs?

A. To continue their education, if not through their employer then through self-study. To be open to all opportunities in the automotive field to include management, parts, or training opportunities. To be a professional and take pride in their career of choice and to portray a positive image.

Q. What are the most important personal and professional qualities for teachers? Automotive technology majors?

A. As a teacher:

- You need to take the initiative to seek out new technology and training to keep current as possible.
- Serve as a role model to the students someone who is professional as well as technically proficient.
- Don't be afraid to challenge your students; students will live up to or down to the standards you establish.
- Constantly review and update courses and curriculum as needed to keep current with industry needs.
- Keep in touch with industry needs (advisory committees, National Automobile Dealers Association, industry publications).

As a student:

- Don't be afraid to challenge yourself.
- Seek out learning opportunities.
- Be professional.

Q. What is the employment outlook in the field?

A. The employment outlook is excellent in the field for the quality graduate. These are the ones who look at the field as a profession. Employers are looking for smart people just like every other field. It takes a lot more discipline, commitment, and organization to be a truly successful technician and problem solver. There are also many opportunities in related areas such as parts, management, and related aftermarket jobs.

Test Drivers

OVERVIEW

Test drivers drive, evaluate, and grade new automobiles and other vehicles before they are made available for sale to the public. They spend many hours driving their assigned model in various driving situations, climates, and speeds. As members of a new product development team, test drivers make suggestions for specific alterations to the car's design, function, and performance. Test drivers are employed by auto manufacturers worldwide, though some may work for contractors specializing in automotive testing or development. Others work as automobile writers and reviewers for trade publications.

HISTORY

There has been a need for test drivers to ensure that vehicles perform well, are safe, and meet other performance criteria ever since the first automobile was manufactured in the late 1800s. In the early days of the automotive industry, cars were tested by engineers, designers, and automotive company owners.

Early test drives were often conducted on the streets of Detroit, Michigan, the headquarters of many automotive manufacturers (many are still located there today). Charles B. King, an automotive industry pioneer, became the first person in the United States to test drive a gasoline-powered automobile on American streets (in Detroit) on March 6, 1896. The *Detroit Free Press* commented the next morning: "The first horseless carriage seen in this city was out on the streets last night. It is the invention of Charles B. King, a Detroiter, and its progress up down Woodward Avenue about 11 o'clock caused a deal of comment, people crowding around it so that its progress was impeded. The apparatus seemed to work all right, and went at the rate of five or six miles an hour at an even rate of speed."

As competition between automotive manufacturers grew and more models were produced, a need emerged for specially trained drivers who could assess the performance of vehicles under a variety of road conditions. Much of this testing took place on the highways and byways of America—allowing the public, as well as automotive competitors, to witness great successes and failures.

It soon became clear that while road testing was important, there was also a need for private testing grounds where automotive companies could test their vehicles under controlled conditions and in secret.

In 1924, General Motors established the first private proving ground, or test track, in the industry in Milford, Michigan. Other companies such as Packard, Studebaker, and Nash (later American Motors) soon followed with their own proving grounds.

Approximately two dozen proving tracks are in operation today in the United States, and test drivers continue to play an important role in the automotive industry—testing vehicles on these tracks as well as public roads and highways.

THE JOB

Automobiles have certainly come a long way in the last few decades. They run smoother, faster, and have more bells and whistles with each new model. However, before auto manufacturers can make new models available to the public, they must ensure that all new features and improvements are safe and reliable. Test drivers are employed by auto manufacturers to drive, evaluate, and grade new cars.

Their work varies depending on the task at hand. Test drivers may be assigned to evaluate the vehicle's dynamics on different types of roads. To gauge the car's performance and handling in high traffic, the driver may travel on highways. Rural or winding roads are often used to test how the car hugs curves and sharp turns, or its handling on rough terrain. Sometimes the driver may use controlled situations such as a closed airport runway, test track, or racing oval to test the car's performance and mileage accumulation at extreme speeds of 150 mph or more.

Test drivers also monitor for any problems and malfunctions with the car's mechanics such as the engine, steering, and brake systems. The driver may take note of any changes in the power and pickup during different stages of the test.

Durability is another component of a driving test. Drivers observe the wear of the car's brakes, tires, bumpers, and other systems with time and usage. Often the car is driven through severe conditions such as damaged roads, inclement weather, and chemicals to test the NVH (noise, vibration, and harshness) engineering, strength of tires and their alignment, shock absorbers, or paint finish.

Test drivers also evaluate the car's ergonomics. They note the comfort of seats, positioning of the steering wheel, and accessibility of other controls ranging from turn signals, to heater and air-conditioning controls, to the car's navigation tools (such as a Global Positioning System [GPS] receiver). Drivers provide feedback on options such as the number and location of cup holders, vanity mirrors, or storage bins. Once testing is complete, drivers may meet with a team of engineers or members of the product development department to make specific changes or alterations. Test drivers may spend years working to help bring a concept design from prototype to an actual product for general consumption.

Test drivers may also participate in special tests to gauge driver fatigue or performance as a result of sleep deprivation or distractions such as cell phone usage or texting. Some auto manufacturers may use professional test drivers to participate in advertising campaigns, company videos, press release photos, or product brochures.

Test drivers can also find employment as writers and editors at publications serving the automobile industry such as *Motor Trend* or *Car and Driver*. Test drivers working in this capacity review new models of cars and compare or evaluate them against similar models offered by other manufacturers. Auto manufacturers loan publications new car models for a short period of time—usually a week. Drivers are allowed to use these cars as they would their own vehicle, keeping notes on their performance. Sometimes, drivers are allowed to drive a model for up to a year to review the car's long-term functionality and reliability.

Test drivers who are employed in publishing often have access to new car models a few months before the general public to allow for the lead time needed for writing, editing, and publishing the review. Auto manufacturers try to maintain good relationships with trade publications as a favorable review is valuable for future car sales.

REQUIREMENTS

High School

Taking auto mechanics courses is a great way to prepare for a career in test driving. It's important to know the mechanics of a car before pushing it to its limits. You'll also want to do well in your driver's education program as test drivers put safety and rules of the road before speed during any driving test.

Test drivers need strong communication skills to be able to convey their test data and observations to team members after every test. You can hone these skills by taking speech or writing classes. Take writing class or any classes that require writing projects—especially if you want to work on the editorial side of auto test driving.

Postsecondary Training
Many successful test drivers are mechanical engineers with a background in automotive engineering. Others have degrees in automotive technology. Additional classes in auto design or manufacturing will also be helpful. If you aspire to write for an industry trade magazine, a degree in journalism, while not necessary, will give you an edge over other employment candidates.

Certification and Licensing
A valid driver's license is a prerequisite for employment in this field, as well as a clean driving record.

One major automotive manufacturer, Ford Motor Company, offers an in-house certification program to ensure that its drivers are property trained and able to handle vehicles at top speeds. The Electronic Driver Certification Tracking System, EDCERTS, is a four-tiered program that qualifies drivers at various skills, tracks, and speeds. Tier 1 is equivalent to public road driving. Tier 2, according to Ford, "is designed for a Ford engineer to drive a vehicle and simultaneously record objective and subjective data for a procedural test measurement." Tier 3 drivers have the ability to "drive at or close to its ultimate limit and road holding capability during chassis development tests to allow a rational assessment and analysis of its behavior." Tier 4, the highest level, certifies drivers to perform extreme maneuvers on any type of track or road at speeds of 200 mph or higher.

Other Requirements
A good test driver will know the mechanics of a car—its power-to-weight ratio, how quickly it changes gears, and how an engine reacts and sounds at various levels of performance. This knowledge is essential in identifying the strengths and weaknesses of a car's design. Test drivers must have a high tolerance for long periods behind the wheel. They often spend many hours driving their assigned cars in difficult situations and at top speeds. Drivers need to

stay focused, have presence of mind, and excellent reflexes to avoid potentially dangerous accidents and crashes

A passion for cars and expert driving abilities are not the only skills needed for this career. Test drivers working on the editorial side must have, along with automotive expertise, the ability to write proficiently. While a journalism background is not a prerequisite for this job, candidates with a writing background will certainly have an edge.

EXPLORING

If you are of age, get your driver's license to gain experience driving on roads and highways. If you are still too young for a driver's license, don't despair as you can hone your driving skills in other ways. Visit a go-karting venue and test your driving performance navigating around other drivers and tricky hairpin turns. Computer and video driving-oriented games will also provide a good introduction to the field.

As you get older, you may want to tinker around with your own car. It's a great way to know how a finely tuned car works and runs. Don't forget to browse trade publications such as *Road & Track* (http://www.roadandtrack.com) for car and performance reviews—you'll become familiar with what drivers look for when testing a new model.

Another way to explore this industry is by attending auto shows. You will be able to see new vehicles, as well as prototypes of cars of the future.

EMPLOYERS

Test drivers are employed by major auto manufacturers. Coveted spots include working as high performance drivers for the Big Three automakers—Ford, Chrysler, and General Motors—though many test drivers vie for positions with major foreign manufacturers such as BMW, Toyota, and Ferrari. Some test drivers are employed by automotive publishing companies.

STARTING OUT

Don't expect to be drag racing a Ford GT Supercar on a closed airstrip on your first day of work. Rather, you may be asked to perform basic tests on how well individual systems work, such as the heating and cooling system or the braking system. Or you may assist in setting up a racing course or other testing site. New test drivers are often assigned lower-end cars, or less demanding test routes such as highways or local roads.

ADVANCEMENT

With enough experience, test drivers may be promoted to head driver for an auto manufacturer. Head drivers often test the higher end, luxury models or may be asked to race a manufacturer's concept or muscle car models. Seeking employment at a larger manufacturer or one specializing in exotic cars, such as Ferrari or Aston Martin, is another form of career advancement.

Test drivers working in the publishing industry can find employment with larger magazines, or may seek additional freelance opportunities for Web sites, e-zines, or local papers.

EARNINGS

The U.S. Department of Labor (USDL) does not provide salary information for test drivers. Some test drivers have backgrounds in mechanical engineering. The USDL reports that mechanical engineers employed in motor vehicle parts manufacturing earned mean annual wages of $70,090 in 2006. Salaries for all mechanical engineers ranged from less than $44,170 to $104,900 or more in 2006.

Writers earned salaries that ranged from less than $25,430 to more than $97,700 in 2006, according to the USDL. Earnings of technical writers ranged from less than $35,520 to $91,720 or more.

Benefits for full-time workers include vacation and sick time, health, and sometimes dental, insurance, and pension or 401(k) plans. Self-employed test drivers must provide their own benefits.

WORK ENVIRONMENT

Test drivers spend the majority of their work day behind the wheel of a car. They are often assigned to drive various types of roads to gauge the car's performance in different situations. Travel is sometimes necessary if the car is manufactured abroad. After a performance test, drivers may meet other team members in an office setting to give reports or brainstorm new alterations. Test drivers writing for a trade publication may take notes during performance testing for use when writing their articles or new product reviews.

Work conditions can occasionally be hazardous. Test drivers often drive their vehicles at top speeds in difficult terrain or less-than-optimal weather conditions. It's important that drivers take every step to protect themselves from injury by wearing seat belts or other protective gear such as helmets, driving gloves, and fireproof clothing.

OUTLOOK

Automobile manufacturers will continue to create new models and improve upon existing vehicles, making them faster, more manageable, and better performing. New models must be thoroughly tested before being made available to the public, so employment opportunities for test drivers will continue to be good—although this is a very small field. Trade magazines will also continue to need good writers with knowledge of the industry and automotive technology for their print publications and Web sites.

FOR MORE INFORMATION

For information on careers in the automotive industry, contact
SAE International
400 Commonwealth Drive
Warrendale, PA 15096-0001
Tel: 877-606-7323
http://automobile.sae.org

For information on a career as a test driver and test-driving facilities, contact the following automotive companies:
BMW
http://www.bmw.com

Chrysler LLC
http://www.chrysler.com

Ford Motor Company
http://www.ford.com

General Motors Corporation
http://www.gm.com

Toyota Motor Sales
http://www.toyota.com

Welders and Welding Technicians

OVERVIEW

Welders operate a variety of special equipment to join metal parts together permanently, usually using heat and sometimes pressure. They work on constructing and repairing automobiles, aircraft, ships, buildings, bridges, highways, appliances, and many other metal structures and manufactured products. *Welding technicians* are the link between the welder and the engineer and work to improve a wide variety of welding processes. As part of their duties, they may supervise, inspect, and find applications for the welding processes. Approximately 28,000 welders and related workers are employed in the motor vehicle and parts manufacturing industry.

HISTORY

Although some welding techniques were used more than 1,000 years ago in forging iron blades by hand, modern welding processes were first employed in the latter half of the 1800s. From experimental beginnings, the pioneers in this field developed a wide variety of innovative processes. These included resistance welding, invented in 1877, in which an electric current is sent through metal parts in contact. Electrical resistance and pressure melt the metal at the area of contact. Gas welding, also developed in the same era, is a relatively simple process using a torch that burns a gas such as acetylene to create enough heat to melt and fuse metal parts. Oxyacetylene welding, a version of this process developed a few years later, is a common welding process still used today. Arc welding, first used commercially in 1889, relies on an electric arc to generate heat. Thermite welding, which fuses metal pieces with the intense heat of a chemical reaction, was first used around 1900.

In the last century, the sudden demand for vehicles and armaments and a growing list of industrial uses for welding that resulted from the two world wars have spurred researchers to keep improving welding processes and also have encouraged the development of numerous new processes. Today, more than 80 different types of welding and welding-related processes are in use. Some of the newer processes include laser-beam welding and electron-beam welding.

THE JOB

Robotic technology perform much of the welding processes that are necessary in the motor and vehicle parts manufacturing industry, but welders are still needed to fix mistakes that have occurred during manufacturing and weld materials in processes that cannot easily be automated.

Welders use various kinds of equipment and processes to create the heat and pressure needed to melt the edges of metal pieces in a controlled fashion so that the pieces may be joined permanently. The processes can be grouped into three categories. The arc welding process derives heat from an electric arc between two electrodes or between an electrode and the workpiece. The gas welding process produces heat by burning a mixture of oxygen and some other combustible gas, such as acetylene or hydrogen. The resistance welding process obtains heat from pressure and resistance by the workpiece to an electric current. The arc and gas methods can also be used to cut, gouge, or finish metal.

Depending on which of these processes and equipment they use, welders may be designated *arc welders*, *gas welders*, or *acetylene welders*. Or they may be *combination welders*, meaning they use a combination of gas and arc welding, or *welding machine operators*, meaning they operate machines that use an arc welding process, electron-beam welding process, laser-beam welding process, or friction welding process. Other workers in the welding field include *resistance machine welders*; *oxygen cutters*, who use gas torches to cut or trim metals; and *arc cutters*, who use an electric arc to cut or trim metals.

Skilled welders usually begin by planning and laying out their work based on drawings, blueprints, or other specifications. Using their working knowledge of the properties of the metal, they determine the proper sequence of operations needed for the job. They may work with steel, stainless steel, cast iron, bronze, aluminum, nickel, and other metals and alloys. Metal pieces to be welded may be in a variety of positions, such as flat, vertical, horizontal, or overhead.

In the manual arc welding process (the most commonly used method), welders grasp a holder containing a suitable electrode and adjust the electric current supplied to the electrode. Then they strike an arc (an electric discharge across a gap) by touching the electrode to the metal. Next, they guide the electrode along the metal seam to be welded, allowing sufficient time for the heat of the arc to melt the metal. The molten metal from the electrode is deposited in the joint and, together with the molten metal edges of the base metal, solidifies to form a solid connection. Welders determine the correct kind of electrode to use based on the job specifications and their knowledge of the materials.

In gas welding, welders melt the metal edges with an intensely hot flame from the combustion of fuel gases in welding torches. First, they obtain the proper types of torch tips and welding rods, which are rods of a filler metal that goes into the weld seam. They adjust the regulators on the tanks of fuel gases, such as oxygen and acetylene, and they light the torch. To obtain the proper size and quality of flame, welders adjust the gas valves on the torch and hold the flame against the metal until it is hot enough. Then they apply the welding rod to the molten metal to supply the extra filler needed to complete the weld.

Maintenance welders, another category of welding workers, may use any of the various welding techniques. They travel to construction sites, utility installations, and other locations to make on-site repairs to metalwork.

Some workers in the welding field do repetitive production tasks using automatic welding equipment. In general, automatic welding is not used where there are critical safety and strength requirements. The surfaces that these welders work on are usually in only one position. Resistance machine welders often work in the mass production of parts, doing the same welding operations repeatedly. To operate the welding machine, they first make adjustments to control the electric current and pressure and then feed in and align the workpieces. After completing the welding operation, welders remove the work from the machine. Welders must constantly monitor the process to make sure that the machine is producing the proper weld.

To cut metal, oxygen cutters may use hand-guided torches or machine-mounted torches. They direct the flame of burning oxygen and fuel gas onto the area to be cut until it melts. Then, an additional stream of gas is released from the torch, which cuts the metal along previously marked lines. Arc cutters follow a similar procedure in their work, except that they use an electric arc as the source of heat. As in oxygen cutting, an additional stream of gas may be released when cutting the metal.

Welding technicians fill positions as *supervisors, inspectors, experimental technicians, sales technicians, assistants to welding engineers,* and *welding analysts* and *estimators.* Some technicians work in research facilities, where they help engineers test and evaluate newly developed welding equipment, metals, and alloys. When new equipment is being developed or old equipment improved, they conduct experiments on it, evaluate the data, and then make recommendations to engineers. Other welding technicians, who work in the field, inspect welded joints and conduct tests to ensure that welds meet company standards, national code requirements, and customer job specifications. These technicians record the results, prepare and submit reports to welding engineers, and conduct welding personnel certification tests according to national code requirements.

Some beginning welding technicians are employed as *welding operators.* They perform manual, automatic, or semiautomatic welding jobs. They set up work, read blueprints and welding-control symbols, and follow specifications set up for a welded product.

As *welding inspectors,* welding technicians judge the quality of incoming materials, such as electrodes, and of welding work being done. They accept or reject pieces of work according to required standards set forth in codes and specifications. A welding inspector must be able to read blueprints, interpret requirements, and have a knowledge of testing equipment and methods.

Closely related to this work is that of the *welding qualification technician.* This person keeps records of certified welders and supervises tests for the qualification of welding operators.

Other welding technicians work as *welding process-control technicians.* These technicians set up the procedures for welders to follow in various production jobs. They specify welding techniques, types of filler wire to be used, ranges for welding electrodes, and time estimates. Welding technicians also provide instructions concerning welding symbols on blueprints, use of jigs and fixtures, and inspection of products.

Equipment maintenance and *sales technicians* work out of welding supply houses. They set up equipment sold by their company, train welding operators to use it, and troubleshoot for customers.

REQUIREMENTS

High School

High school graduates are preferred for trainee positions for skilled jobs. Useful high school courses for prospective welders include mathematics, blueprint reading, mechanical drawing, applied physics, and shop. If possible, the shop courses should cover the basics of welding and working with electricity.

Postsecondary Training

Many welders learn their skills through formal training programs in welding, such as those available in many community colleges, technical institutes, trade schools, and the armed forces. Some programs are short term and narrow in focus, while others provide several years of thorough preparation for a variety of jobs.

A high school diploma or its equivalent is required for admission into these programs. Beginners can also learn welding skills in on-the-job training programs. The length of such training programs ranges from several days or weeks for jobs requiring few skills to a period of one to three years for skilled jobs. Trainees often begin as helpers to experienced workers, doing very simple tasks. As they learn, they are given more challenging work. To learn some skilled jobs, trainees supplement their on-the-job training with formal classroom instruction in technical aspects of the trade.

Various programs sponsored by federal, state, and local governments provide training opportunities in some areas. These training programs, which usually stress the fundamentals of welding, may be in the classroom or on the job and last from a few weeks to a year. Apprenticeship programs also offer training. Apprenticeships that teach a range of metalworking skills, including the basics of welding, are run by trade unions such as the International Association of Machinists and Aerospace Workers.

Certification or Licensing

To do welding work where the strength of the weld is a critical factor (such as in automobiles, aircraft, bridges, boilers, or high-pressure pipelines), welders may have to pass employer tests or standardized examinations for certification by government agencies or professional and technical associations.

Other Requirements

Employers generally prefer to hire applicants who are in good enough physical condition to bend, stoop, and work in awkward positions.

A worker welds a vehicle at a manufacturing plant. *(Zheng Xianzhang, Panorama, The Image Works)*

Applicants also need manual dexterity, good eye-hand coordination, and good eyesight, as well as patience and the ability to concentrate for extended periods as they work on a task.

Many people in welding and related occupations belong to one of the following unions: International Association of Machinists and Aerospace Workers; International Brotherhood of Boilermakers, Iron Ship Builders, Blacksmiths, Forgers and Helpers; International Union, United Automobile, Aerospace and Agricultural Implement Workers of America; United Association of Journeymen and Apprentices of the Plumbing and Pipe Fitting Industry of the United States and Canada; or United Electrical, Radio, and Machine Workers of America.

EXPLORING

With the help of a teacher or a guidance counselor, students may be able to arrange to visit a workplace where they can observe welders or welding machine operators on the job. Ideally, such a visit can provide a chance to see several welding processes and various kinds of welding work and working conditions, as well as an opportunity to talk with welders about their work.

EMPLOYERS

Workers in welding occupations work in a variety of settings. About two-thirds of welders are employed in manufacturing plants that produce motor vehicles and parts, ships, boilers, machinery, appliances, and other metal products. Most of the remaining welders work for repair shops or construction companies that build bridges, large buildings, pipelines, and similar metal structures. All welding machine operators work in manufacturing industries. Approximately 28,000 welders and related workers are employed in the motor vehicle and parts manufacturing industry. Employers include the Big Three U.S. automobile makers (Chrysler LLC, Ford Motor Company, and General Motors), major foreign automakers that have factories or divisions in the United States (BMW, Honda, Hyundai, Mercedes-Benz, Nissan, Toyota), as well as any of the thousands of private manufacturing companies.

STARTING OUT

Graduates of good training programs in welding often receive help in finding jobs through their schools' career services offices. The classified ads sections of newspapers often carry listings of local job openings. Information about openings for trainee positions, apprenticeships, and government training programs, as well as jobs for skilled workers, may be available through the local offices of the state employment service and local offices of unions that organize welding workers. Job seekers also can apply directly to the personnel offices at automotive manufacturers that hire welders.

ADVANCEMENT

Advancement usually depends on acquiring additional skills. Workers who gain experience and learn new processes and techniques are increasingly valuable to their employers, and they may be promoted to positions as supervisors, inspectors, or welding instructors. With further formal technical training, welders may qualify for welding technician jobs. Some experienced welders go into business for themselves and open their own welding and repair shops.

Welding technicians can become *welding supervisors* and take on the responsibility of assigning jobs to workers and showing them how the tasks should be performed. They must supervise job performance and ensure that operations are performed correctly and economically. Other technicians become *welding instructors*, teaching welding theory, techniques, and related processes. Finally, some technicians advance to the position of *welding production manager*, responsible for all aspects of welding production: equipment, materials, process control, inspection, and cost control.

EARNINGS

According to the U.S. Department of Labor, welders employed in motor vehicle manufacturing earned median wages of $20.62 an hour in 2006 ($42,890 annually). Those employed in motor vehicle parts manufacturing earned $15.14 an hour in 2006 (or $31,491 annually). Salaries for all welders ranged from less than $20,970 to $46,800 or more. In addition to wages, employers often provide fringe benefits, such as health insurance plans, paid vacation time, paid sick time, and pension plans. Salaries for welding technicians vary according to the individual's function and level of education as well as the geographic location of the business.

WORK ENVIRONMENT

Welders may spend their workday inside in well-ventilated and well-lighted shops and factories, outside at a construction site, or in confined spaces, such as in an underground tunnel or inside a large storage tank that is being built. Welding jobs can involve working in uncomfortable positions. Sometimes welders work for short periods in booths that are built to contain sparks and glare. In some jobs, workers must repeat the same procedure over and over.

Welders often encounter hazardous conditions and may need to wear goggles, helmets with protective faceplates, protective clothing, safety shoes, and other gear to prevent burns and other injuries. Many metals give off toxic gases and fumes when heated, and workers must be careful to avoid exposure to such harmful substances. Other potential dangers include explosions from mishandling combustible gases and electric shock. Workers in this field must learn the safest ways of carrying out welding work and always pay attention to safety procedures. Various trade and safety organizations have developed rules for welding procedures, safety practices, and health precautions that can minimize the risks of the job. Operators of automatic welding machines are exposed to fewer hazards than manual welders and cutters, and they usually need to use less protective gear.

OUTLOOK

Employment for welders in motor vehicle and parts manufacturing is expected to decline through 2016, according to the U.S. Department of Labor (USDL). In automotive manufacturing, the trend toward increasing automation, including more use of welding robots, is expected to decrease the demand for manual welders and increase the demand for welding machine operators.

Overall employment in welding and related occupations is expected to grow more slowly than the average for all occupations through 2014, according to the USDL. Plenty of opportunities should exist for skilled welders, since many employers have difficulties in finding qualified applicants. Most job openings will develop when experienced workers leave their jobs. During periods when the economy is in a slowdown, many workers in construction and manufacturing, including some welders, may be laid off.

FOR MORE INFORMATION

For more information about becoming a welder, contact the following organizations:

American Welding Society
550 Northwest LeJeune Road
Miami, FL 33126-5649
Tel: 800-443-9353
http://www.aws.org

International Association of Machinists and Aerospace Workers
9000 Machinists Place
Upper Marlboro, MD 20772-2687
Tel: 301-967-4500
Email: websteward@goiam.org
http://www.iamaw.org

Writers, Automotives

OVERVIEW

Writers express, edit, promote, and interpret ideas and facts in written form for books, magazines, trade journals, newspapers, technical studies and reports, company newsletters, radio and television broadcasts, and advertisements. They report, analyze, and interpret facts, events, and personalities; review products and services; and persuade the general public to choose or favor certain goods and services. Automotive writers specialize in writing about the automotive industry—from new cars and automotive manufacturers, to technological developments that are making cars more eco-friendly, to the history of the industry and many other topics. Approximately 184,000 salaried writers, authors, and technical writers are employed in the United States. Automotive writers make up only a small percentage of this number.

HISTORY

The skill of writing has existed for thousands of years. Papyrus fragments with writing by ancient Egyptians date from about 3000 B.C., and archaeological findings show that the Chinese had developed books by about 1300 B.C. A number of technical obstacles had to be overcome before printing and the profession of writing evolved. Books of the Middle Ages were copied by hand on parchment. The ornate style that marked these works helped ensure their rarity. Also, few people were able to read.

The development of the printing press by Johannes Gutenberg in the middle of the 15th century and the liberalism of the Protestant Reformation, which encouraged a wide range of publications, greater literacy, and the creation of a number of works of literary merit, prompted the development of the publishing industry. The first authors worked directly with printers.

The modern publishing age began in the 18th century. Printing became mechanized, and the novel, magazine, and newspaper developed.

Advances in the printing trades, photoengraving, retailing, and the availability of capital produced a boom in newspapers and magazines in the 19th century. Further mechanization in the printing field, such as the use of the Linotype machine, high-speed rotary presses, and special color reproduction processes, set the stage for still further growth in the book, newspaper, and magazine industry.

In addition to the print media, the broadcasting industry has contributed to the development of the professional writer. Film, radio, and television are sources of entertainment, information, and education that provide employment for thousands of writers.

Writers have been extolling the virtues of automobiles and related topics ever since German automobile pioneers Karl Benz and Gottlieb Daimler developed a gasoline-powered internal combustion engine in the 1880s. As the auto industry developed, cars went from novelties to must-haves (for a population that was rapidly expanding to the suburbs and beyond) to status symbols for the rich and objects of adoration for the dedicated hobbyist. Books, magazines, and other media that covered this fast-growing industry soon developed to meet the interest of the car-hungry public. Three of the oldest and most popular automotive magazines are *Motor Sport* (which was founded as the *Brooklands Gazette* in 1924), *Motor Trend* (which was first published in 1949), and *Car and Driver* (which was founded as *Sports Cars Illustrated* in 1955). These magazines are still published today.

The International Motor Press Association was founded nearly 50 years ago to represent the professional interests of automotive writers and public relations specialists. Other well-known professional associations for automotive writers include the American Auto Racing Writers and Broadcasters Association, and the National Motorsports Press Association.

THE JOB

Automotive writers work in the field of communications. Specifically, they deal with the written word, whether it is destined for the printed page, broadcast, or computer screen. The nature of their work is as varied as the materials they produce: books, magazines, trade journals, newspapers, technical reports, company newsletters and other publications, advertisements, speeches, and scripts for radio and television broadcast. Automotive writers develop ideas and write for all media.

Staff writers are employed by automotive magazines and newspapers to write news stories, feature articles, and columns about a wide variety of subjects including new car models and features, industry sales trends, and well-known workers in the field. First they come up with an idea for an article from their own interests or are assigned a topic by an editor. The topic is of relevance to the particular publication; for example, a writer for *AutoExec* magazine, which is geared toward dealership owners, might be assigned to write an article on how rising gas prices are affecting new car sales. Then writers begin gathering as much information as possible about the subject through library research, interviews, the Internet, observation, and other methods. They keep extensive notes from which they will draw material for their project. Once the material has been organized and arranged in logical sequence, writers prepare a written outline. The process of developing a piece of writing is exciting, although it can also involve detailed and solitary work. After researching an idea, a writer might discover that a different perspective or related topic would be more effective, entertaining, or marketable.

Columnists or *commentators* analyze news and social issues. They write about events from the standpoint of their own experience or opinion. They might write a column about a recent auto show they attended, the relaunch of a classic car series, or a key player in the industry, such as William Clay Ford Jr., the executive chairman of the board of directors of Ford Motor Company.

Editorial writers write on topics of public interest, and their comments, consistent with the viewpoints and policies of their employers, are intended to stimulate or mold public opinion. A columnist for an automotive association publication, for example, might write a column detailing his or her opposition to new laws enacted by the federal government that limit the growth of the automotive industry.

Corporate writers are employed by large automotive companies such as Ford and General Motors, as well as many smaller companies in the automotive industry. They write news releases, annual reports, speeches for the company head, or public relations materials. Typically they are assigned a topic with length requirements for a given project. They may receive raw research materials, such as statistics, and they are expected to conduct additional research, including personal interviews. These writers must be able to write quickly and accurately on short deadlines, while also working with people whose primary job is not in the communications field. The written work is submitted to a supervisor and often a legal department for approval; rewrites are a normal part of this job.

Automotive copywriters write copy that is primarily designed to sell automobiles, trucks, and other vehicles. Their work appears as advertisements in newspapers, magazines, and other publications or as commercials on radio and television broadcasts. Sales and marketing representatives first provide information on the product and help determine the style and length of the copy. Copywriters conduct additional research and interviews; to formulate an effective approach, they study advertising trends and review surveys of consumer preferences. Armed with this information, copywriters write a draft that is submitted to the account executive and the client for approval. The copy is often returned for correction and revision until everyone involved is satisfied. Copywriters, like corporate writers, may also write articles, bulletins, news releases, sales letters, speeches, and other related informative and promotional material. Many copywriters are employed in advertising agencies. They also may work for public relations firms or in communications departments of automotive companies and large dealerships.

Technical writers can be divided into two main groups: those who convert technical information into material for the general public, and those who convey technical information between professionals. Technical writers in the first group may prepare automotive service manuals or handbooks, instruction or repair booklets, or sales literature or brochures; those in the second group may write research reports, contract specifications, or research abstracts.

Some automotive writers may work as *test drivers* for publications serving the automobile industry such as *Motor Trend* or *Car and Driver*. Test drivers working in this capacity review new models of cars and compare or evaluate them against similar models offered by other manufacturers.

When working on assignment, writers usually submit their outlines to an editor or other company representative for approval. Then they write a first draft, trying to put the material into words that will have the desired effect on their audience. They often rewrite or polish sections of the material as they proceed, always searching for just the right way of imparting information or expressing an idea or opinion. A manuscript may be reviewed, corrected, and revised numerous times before a final copy is submitted. Even after that, an editor may request additional changes.

Automotive writers often have an educational background that allows them to give critical interpretations or analyses. For example, a writer for a newspaper may have a degree in automotive

Automotive journalists inspect the Geely 7151 CD at the North American International Auto Show. *(Jim West Photography)*

technology, engineering, or design and can interpret new ideas in the field for the average reader.

Automotive writers can be employed either as in-house staff or as freelancers. Pay varies according to experience and the position, but freelancers must provide their own office space and equipment such as computers and fax machines. Freelancers also are responsible for keeping tax records, sending out invoices, negotiating contracts, and providing their own health insurance.

REQUIREMENTS

High School

While in high school, build a broad educational foundation by taking courses in English, literature, foreign languages, history, general science, social studies, computer science, and typing. The ability to type is almost a requisite for all positions in the communications field, as is familiarity with computers. If you plan to work in the automotive industry, it is a good idea to learn as much as you can about the field by taking automotive-related courses.

Postsecondary Training

Competitive writing jobs almost always demand the background of a college education. Many employers prefer you have a broad liberal arts background or majors in English, literature, history, philosophy, or one of the social sciences. Other employers desire communications or journalism training in college. Occasionally a master's degree in a specialized writing field may be required. A number of schools offer courses in journalism, and some of them offer courses or majors in book publishing, publication management, and newspaper and magazine writing.

In addition to formal course work, most employers look for practical writing experience. If you have served on high school or college newspapers, yearbooks, or literary magazines, or if you have worked for small community newspapers or radio stations, even in an unpaid position, you will be an attractive candidate. Many book publishers, magazines, newspapers, and radio and television stations have summer internship programs that provide valuable training if you want to learn about the publishing and broadcasting businesses. Interns do many simple tasks, such as running errands and answering phones, but some may be asked to perform research, conduct interviews, or even write some minor pieces.

Writers who specialize in the automotive industry may need degrees, concentrated course work, or experience in specific subject areas. This applies frequently to engineering, industrial design, business, or one of the sciences. Also, technical communications is a degree now offered at many universities and colleges.

Other Requirements
To be a writer, you should be creative and able to express ideas clearly, have a broad general knowledge, be skilled in research techniques, and be computer literate. Other assets include curiosity, persistence, initiative, resourcefulness, and an accurate memory. For some jobs—on a newspaper, for example, where the activity is hectic and deadlines are short—the ability to concentrate and produce under pressure is essential.

To be successful in the automotive industry, you should have a strong interest in automobiles and related technology.

EXPLORING

As a high school or college student, you can test your interest and aptitude in the field of writing by serving as a reporter or writer on school newspapers, yearbooks, and literary magazines. Various writing courses and workshops will provide the opportunity to sharpen your writing skills.

Small community newspapers and local radio stations often welcome contributions from outside sources, although they may not have the resources to pay for them. Jobs in bookstores, magazine shops, and even newsstands will offer you a chance to become familiar with various publications.

You can also obtain information on writing as a career by visiting local newspapers, publishers, or radio and television stations and interviewing some of the writers who work there. Career conferences and other guidance programs frequently include speakers on the entire field of communications from local or national organizations.

If you are interested in becoming an automotive writer, read magazines and books about the field. Magazines such as *Car Design News* (http://www.cardesignnews.com), *Automotive Design & Production* (http://www.autofieldguide.com), *AutoExec* (http://www.autoexecmag.com), *Road & Track* (http://www.roadandtrack.com), and *Car and Driver* (http://www.caranddriver.com) will help you learn more about the field and the topics automotive writers cover. You also try contact one of the writers for these magazines to see if they would be interested in participating in an information interview about their careers.

EMPLOYERS

Approximately 135,000 writers and authors and 49,000 technical writers are currently employed in the United States; only a small percentage of this total are automotive writers. Approximately one-third of salaried writers and editors work in the information sector, which includes newspapers, magazines, book publishers, radio and television broadcasting, software publishers, and Internet businesses. Writers also work for advertising agencies and public relations firms and work on journals and newsletters published by business and nonprofit organizations.

Automotive writers can find employment with one of the Big Three U.S. automobile makers (General Motors, Ford Motor Company, and Chrysler LLC), major foreign automakers that have factories or divisions in the United States (Honda, Nissan, Toyota, Hyundai, BMW, and Mercedes-Benz), as well as any of the thousands of private manufacturing companies.

STARTING OUT

A fair amount of experience is required to gain a high-level position in the field. Most automotive writers start out in entry-level positions. These jobs may be listed with college career services offices, or they may be obtained by applying directly to the employment departments of the individual publishers or broadcasting companies. Graduates who previously served internships with these companies often have the advantage of knowing someone who can give them a personal recommendation. Want ads in newspapers and trade journals are another source for jobs. Because of the competition for positions, however, few vacancies are listed with public or private employment agencies.

Employers in the communications field usually are interested in samples of published writing. These are often assembled in an organized portfolio or scrapbook. Bylined or signed articles are more credible (and, as a result, more useful) than stories whose source is not identified.

Entry-level positions as a *junior writer* usually involve library research, preparation of rough drafts for part or all of a report, cataloging, and other related writing tasks. These are generally carried on under the supervision of a senior writer.

Some technical writers have entered the field after working in public relations departments or as automotive technicians, engineers, or research assistants, then transferring to technical writing as openings occur. Many firms now hire writers directly upon application or recommendation of college professors and career services offices.

Members of the International Motor Press Association can also access job listings at the organization's Web site, http://www.impa.org.

ADVANCEMENT

Most automotive writers find their first jobs as editorial or production assistants. Advancement may be more rapid in small companies, where beginners learn by doing a little bit of everything and may be given writing tasks immediately. In large companies, duties are usually more compartmentalized. Assistants in entry-level positions are assigned such tasks as research, fact checking, and copyrighting, but it generally takes much longer to advance to full-scale writing duties.

Promotion into more responsible positions may come with the assignment of more important articles and stories to write, or it may be the result of moving to another company. Mobility among employees in this field is common. An assistant in one publishing house may switch to an executive position in another. Or a writer may switch to a related field as a type of advancement.

A *technical writer* can be promoted to positions of responsibility by moving from such jobs as *writer* to *technical editor* to *project leader* or *documentation manager.* Opportunities in specialized positions also are possible.

Freelance or self-employed automotive writers earn advancement in the form of larger fees as they gain exposure and establish their reputations.

EARNINGS

In 2006, median annual earnings for salaried writers and authors employed in all fields were $48,640 a year, according to the U.S. Department of Labor. The lowest 10 percent earned less than $25,430, while the highest 10 percent earned $97,700 or more. In book publishing, some specialties pay better than others. Technical writers earned a median salary of $58,050 in 2006, with entry-level salaries averaging around $35,520 a year.

In addition to their salaries, many automotive writers earn some income from freelance work. Part-time freelancers may earn from $5,000 to $15,000 a year. Freelance earnings vary widely. Full-time established freelance writers may earn more than $75,000 a year.

Typical benefits may be available for full-time salaried employees including sick leave, vacation pay, and health, life, and disability insurance. Retirement plans may also be available, and some companies may match employees' contributions. Some companies may also offer stock-option plans.

Freelance writers do not receive benefits and are responsible for their own medical, disability, and life insurance. They do not receive vacation pay, and when they aren't working, they aren't generating income. Retirement plans must also be self-funded and self-directed.

WORK ENVIRONMENT

Working conditions vary for automotive writers. Although their workweek usually runs 35 to 40 hours, many writers work overtime. A publication that is issued frequently has more deadlines closer together, creating greater pressures to meet them. The work is especially hectic on newspapers and at broadcasting companies, which operate seven days a week. Writers often work nights and weekends to meet deadlines or to cover a late-developing story.

Most writers work independently, but they often must cooperate with artists, photographers, rewriters, and advertising people who may have widely differing ideas of how the materials should be prepared and presented.

Physical surroundings range from comfortable private offices, to noisy, crowded newsrooms filled with other workers typing and talking on the telephone, to loud, fume-filled test tracks. Some writers must confine their research to the library or telephone interviews, but others may travel to other cities or countries or to local sites, such as test tracks, auto shows, factories, laboratories, or other offices. Writers who test drive vehicles spend a considerable amount of their workday behind the wheel of a car. These tests may be conducted on a private testing track or on city highways, mountain roads, or in rural settings.

The work is arduous, but most writers are seldom bored. The most difficult element is the continual pressure of deadlines. People who are the most content as writers enjoy and work well with deadline pressure.

OUTLOOK

The employment of all writers is expected to increase at an average rate through 2016, according to the U.S. Department of Labor. Competition for writing jobs has been and will continue to be competitive. The demand for writers by newspapers, periodicals, book publishers, and nonprofit organizations is expected to increase. The growth of online publishing on company Web sites and other online services will also create a demand for many talented writers; those with computer skills will be at an advantage as a result. The fields of advertising and public relations should also provide job opportunities.

Americans have been fascinated with the automobile ever since the first Model T rolled off the production line more than 100 years ago. With countless magazines, books, Web sites, and radio and television shows about cars and the automotive industry, the employment opportunities for writers in the field should continue to be strong.

People entering this field should realize that the competition for jobs is extremely keen. Beginners may have difficulty finding employment. Of the thousands who graduate each year with degrees in English, journalism, communications, and the liberal arts, intending to establish a career as a writer, many turn to other occupations when they find that applicants far outnumber the job openings available. College students would do well to keep this in mind and prepare for an unrelated alternate career in the event they are unable to obtain a position as writer; another benefit of this approach is that they can become qualified as writers in a specialized field. The practicality of preparing for alternate careers is borne out by the fact that opportunities are best in firms that prepare business and trade publications and in technical writing. Job candidates with good writing skills and knowledge of a specialized area such as economics, finance, computer programming, or science will have the best chances of finding jobs.

Potential writers who end up working in a different field may be able to earn some income as freelancers, selling articles, stories, books, and possibly TV and movie scripts, but it is usually difficult for writers to support themselves entirely as independent writers.

FOR MORE INFORMATION

The MPA is a good source of information about internships.
Magazine Publishers of America (MPA)
810 Seventh Avenue, 24th Floor
New York, NY 10019-5873
Tel: 212-872-3700
Email: mpa@magazine.org
http://www.magazine.org

For information on automotive writing careers, contact the following organizations:
American Auto Racing Writers and Broadcasters Association
922 North Pass Avenue
Burbank, CA 91505-2703
Tel: 818-842-7005
http://www.aarwba.org

International Motor Press Association
Tel: 201-750-3533
http://www.impa.org

Motor Press Guild
4561 Colorado Boulevard
Los Angeles, CA 90039-1103
Tel: 310-693-4943
http://www.motorpressguild.org

National Motorsports Press Association
PO Box 500
Darlington, SC 29540-0500
Tel: 843-395-8900
http://www.nmpaonline.com

Western Automotive Journalists
http://www.waj.org

This organization offers student memberships for those interested in opinion writing.
National Conference of Editorial Writers
3899 North Front Street
Harrisburg, PA 17110-1583
Tel: 717-703-3015
Email: ncew@pa-news.org
http://www.ncew.org

This organization for journalists has campus and online chapters.
Society of Professional Journalists
Eugene S. Pulliam National Journalism Center
3909 North Meridian Street
Indianapolis, IN 46208-4011
Tel: 317-927-8000
http://www.spj.org

For information on scholarships and student memberships aimed at those preparing for a career in technical communication, contact
Society for Technical Communication
901 North Stuart Street, Suite 904
Arlington, VA 22203-1822
Tel: 703-522-4114
Email: stc@stc.org
http://www.stc.org

INTERVIEW

Dan Lyons is an automotive writer and photographer based in New York State. (You can learn more about his career by visiting http://lyonsonwheels.com.) Dan discussed the field with the editors of Careers in Focus: Automotives.

Q. How long have you been an automotive writer/photographer? Please tell us about your business.

A. I've been writing about new cars for about 17 years; a writer/photographer of old cars for about 20 years. I began my business as a photographer, not a writer. I had for some time been taking pictures of classic cars and muscle cars that belonged to friends of mine. I decided to try and get my work published, zeroed in on the old car magazines that I liked the best, and started lobbying them to use me as a photographer. Once I'd been successful in doing this for a while, I realized that I'd get more work if I wrote the pieces as well as provided the photography. Giving the editors the whole package removes an impediment to getting published—they don't have to match up a writer and a photographer.

A few years later, I approached my local newspaper about doing car reviews for their weekly automotive insert—something that was locally based and more tailored to their readership than the syndicated reviews that they were running. I started providing new car reviews for them a few weeks later, and have been doing so ever since. That experience in turn has lead to opportunities to write for other publications as well.

So far, I've written six books on cars and provided the photography for more than 70 calendars. I don't know how many road tests I've written over the years.

Q. Why did you decide to become an automotive writer?
A. The business is an extension of my lifelong interest in cars.

Q. What do you like most and least about your job?
A. For someone with a long-standing love of cars, the opportunity to drive the latest vehicles is endlessly interesting. On the old car side of my business, the cars are rolling history. They say a lot about the culture and the times that they were produced in. And, the hobby has some great people in it. I've been privileged to get to know a lot of them over the years.

In terms of difficulties with the profession, publications (print or Web based) tend to come and go, and their respective editorial staff members even more so. Particularly if you freelance, you are constantly building and rebuilding relationships with people that you will be working with.

Q. What advice would you give to high school students who are interested in this career?
A. Learn to type! You'll end up logging a lot of time at the keyboard in this field. The faster you can type, the more seamless will be the flow between your thoughts and their written expression. Study your subject matter, practice your craft, find your voice. The ability to express your thoughts clearly and develop a distinctive style will help distinguish you in a crowded field.

Q. What are the most important professional qualities for automotive writers?

A. Product knowledge, communication skills and, most of all, determination. Lots of people would do this kind of work for little or nothing. If you're going to convince someone that they should hire you instead of them, you need to be good, and you need to be persistent. You also need a hard nose, because it's going to get a door slammed into it frequently, especially as you're starting out.

Q. What has been one of your most interesting and fulfilling experiences as an automotive writer?

A. Being among the first to climb behind the wheel of an interesting new car model never gets old. Having the opportunity to drive on some of the race tracks that you grow up reading about is also fun, and really gives you some perspective on just how good the best drivers are. When everything comes together in photography—a fine car in an interesting setting on a beautiful day—it's one of my absolute favorite things. Seeing classics at close range allows you to appreciate their personalities.

Index

Entries in **boldface** indicate main articles.

A

Accreditation Board for Engineering and Technology
  Technology Accreditation Commission 66
Accrediting Commission of Career Schools and Colleges of Technology 41
acetylene welders. *See* welders and welding technicians
advancement section, explained 4
alternative-fuel technicians. *See* automobile service technicians
American Auto Racing Writers and Broadcasters Association 169
American Driver and Traffic Safety Education Association 104
American International Automobile Dealers 49
American Motor Company 36–37, 153
American Red Cross 135
American Society for Quality 113
American Society of Certified Engineering Technicians 68
American Welding Society 87
arc cutters. *See* welders and welding technicians
arc welders. *See* welders and welding technicians
Ashland Community and Technical College Diesel Technology Program 101–102
assistants to welding engineers. *See* welders and welding technicians
Association of Diesel Specialists 96
AutoExec 170, 174
automobile collision repairers 5–16
  advancement 11–12
  certification or licensing 9
  earnings 12
  educational requirements 9
  employers 11
  employment outlook 13–14
  exploring the field 10
  high school requirements 9
  history 5–6
  interview 15–16
  job, described 6–9
  for more information 14–15
  postsecondary training 9
  requirements 9–10
  starting out 11
  work environment 12–13

automobile detailers 17–24
  advancement 22
  certification or licensing 20
  earnings 22
  educational requirements 19–20
  employers 21
  employment outlook 23
  exploring the field 21
  high school requirements 19–20
  history 17–18
  job, described 18–19
  for more information 23–24
  postsecondary training 20
  requirements 19–20
  starting out 21–22
  work environment 22–23
automobile-radiator mechanics. *See* automobile service technicians
automobile service technicians 36–47
  advancement 44
  certification or licensing 42
  earnings 44
  educational requirements 40–42
  employers 43
  employment outlook 45–46
  exploring the field 42
  high school requirements 40
  history 36–37
  job, described 37–40
  for more information 46–47
  postsecondary training 40–42
  requirements 40–42
  starting out 43–44
  work environment 45
automobile testers. *See* inspectors
Automotive Aftermarket Industry Association 138
Automotive Body Repair News 10, 13
Automotive Careers Today 54
automotive copywriters. *See* writers, automotive
automotive dealership owners and sales managers 48–55
  advancement 53
  certification or licensing 51–52
  earnings 53–54
  educational requirements 50–52
  employers 53
  employment outlook 54–55
  exploring the field 52–53
  facts about dealerships 52
  high school requirements 50
  history 48–49